THE NEW BEING

Also by Paul Tillich

THE SHAKING OF THE FOUNDATIONS
a companion volume to THE NEW BEING

THE
NEW BEING

By

PAUL TILLICH

NEW YORK
CHARLES SCRIBNER'S SONS

To

MARY HEILNER

Preface

THIS BOOK contains sermons which I gave mostly in colleges and universities, especially in Union Theological Seminary, New York, and in Connecticut College, New London, Connecticut, since the publication of the first volume of my sermons *The Shaking of the Foundations*.

The two titles: *The Shaking of the Foundations* and *The New Being* show the relation of the main problems of the first to those of the second volume. *The New Being* is, so to speak, the answer to the questions developed in *The Shaking of the Foundations*.

I want to express my thanks to Miss Mary Heilner to whom this volume is dedicated and who in this as in the first volume helped me to eliminate Germanisms and other stylistic shortcomings and advised me in the organization of the whole book.

In the main, quotations from the Bible are given according to the Revised Standard Version, copyrighted 1946 and 1952, with the kind permission of the copyright owner, Division of Christian Education, National Council of the Churches of Christ in the U. S. A.

P. T.

New York, 1955

Contents

THE NEW BEING

PART I

The New Being as Love

1

"TO WHOM MUCH IS FORGIVEN . . ."

One of the Pharisees asked him to eat with him, and he went into the Pharisee's house, and sat at table. And behold, a woman of the city, who was a sinner, when she learned that he was sitting at table in the Pharisee's house, brought an alabaster flask of ointment, and standing behind him at his feet, weeping, she began to wet his feet with her tears, and wiped them with the hair of her head, and kissed his feet, and anointed them with the ointment. Now when the Pharisee who had invited him saw it, he said to himself, "If this man were a prophet, he would have known who and what sort of woman this is who is touching him, for she is a sinner." And Jesus answering said to him, "Simon, I have something to say to you." And he answered, "What is it, Teacher?" "A certain creditor had two debtors; one owed five hundred denarii, and the other fifty. When they could not pay, he forgave them both. Now which of them will love him more?" Simon answered, "The one, I suppose, to whom he forgave more." And he said to him, "You have judged rightly." Then turning toward the woman he said to Simon, "Do you see this woman? I entered your house, you gave

3

*me no water for my feet, but she has wet my feet
with her tears and wiped them with her hair. You
gave me no kiss, but from the time I came in she has
not ceased to kiss my feet. You did not anoint my
head with oil, but she has anointed my feet with
ointment. Therefore, I tell you, her sins, which are
many, are forgiven, for she loved much; but he who
is forgiven little, loves little."*

LUKE 7:36-47.

THE STORY WE HAVE READ, LIKE THE
parable of the Prodigal Son, is peculiar to the Gospel
of Luke. In this story, as in the parable, someone who
is considered to be a great sinner, by others as well as
by herself, is contrasted with people who are considered to be genuinely righteous. In both cases Jesus is
on the side of the sinner, and therefore He is criticized,
indirectly in the parable by the righteous elder son,
and directly in our story by the righteous Pharisee.

We should not diminish the significance of this attitude of Jesus by asserting that, after all, the sinners
were not as sinful, nor the righteous as righteous as they
were judged to be by themselves and by others. Nothing like this is indicated in the story or in the parable.
The sinners, one a whore and the other the companion
of whores, are not excused by ethical arguments which
would remove the seriousness of the moral demand.
They are not excused by sociological explanations which
would remove their personal responsibility; nor by an
analysis of their unconscious motives which would remove the significance of their conscious decisions; nor

by man's universal predicament which would remove their personal guilt. They are called sinners, simply and without restriction. This does not mean that Jesus and the New Testament writers are unaware of the psychological and sociological factors which determine human existence. They are keenly aware of the universal and inescapable dominion of sin over this world, of the demonic splits in the souls of people, which produce insanity and bodily destruction; of the economic and spiritual misery of the masses. But their awareness of these factors, which have become so decisive for *our* description of man's predicament, does not prevent them from calling the sinners sinners. Understanding does not replace judging. We understand more and better than many generations before us. But our immensely increased insight into the conditions of human existence should not undercut our courage to call wrong wrong. In story and parable the sinners are seriously called sinners.

And in the same way the righteous ones are seriously called righteous. We would miss the spirit of our story if we tried to show that the righteous ones are not truly righteous. The elder son in the parable did what he was supposed to do. He does not feel that he has done anything wrong nor does his father tell him so. His righteousness is not questioned—nor is the righteousness of Simon, the Pharisee. His lack of love toward Jesus is not reproached as a lack of righteousness, but it is derived from the fact that little is forgiven to him.

Such righteousness is not easy to attain. Much self-control, hard discipline, and continuous self-observation are needed. Therefore, we should not despise the

righteous ones. In the traditional Christian view, the
Pharisees have become representatives of everything
evil, but in their time they were the pious and morally
zealous ones. Their conflict with Jesus was not simply
a conflict between right and wrong; it was, above all,
the conflict between an old and sacred tradition and a
new reality which was breaking into it and depriving
it of ultimate significance. It was not only a moral conflict—it was also a tragic one, foreshadowing the tragic
conflict between Christianity and Judaism in all suc-
ceeding generations, including our own. The Pharisees
—and this we should not forget—were the guardians of
the law of God in their time.

The Pharisees can be compared with other groups of
righteous ones. We can compare them, for example,
with a group that has played a tremendous role in the
history of this country—the Puritans. The name itself,
like the name Pharisee, indicates separation from the
impurities of the world. The Puritans would certainly
have judged the attitude of Jesus to the whore as Simon
the Pharisee did. And we should not condemn them for
this judgment nor distort their picture in our loose talk
about them. Like the Pharisees, they were the guardians
of the law of God in their time.

And what about our time? It has been said, and not
without justification, that the Protestant churches have
become middle-class churches because of the way in
which their members interpret Christianity, practically
as well as theoretically. Such criticism points to their
active adherence to their churches, to their well-estab-
lished morality, to their charitable works. They are
righteous—they would have been called so by Jesus.

And certainly they would have joined Simon the Pharisee and the Puritans in criticizing the attitude of Jesus
towards the woman in our story. And again I say, we
should not condemn them for this. They take their
religious and moral obligations seriously. They, like the
Pharisees and the Puritans, are guardians of the law of
God in our time.

The sinners are seriously called sinners and the righteous ones are seriously called righteous. Only if this is
clearly seen can the depth and the revolutionary power
of Jesus' attitude be understood. He takes the side of
the sinner against the righteous although He does not
doubt the validity of the law, the guardians of which
the righteous are. Here we approach a mystery which
is the mystery of the Christian message itself, in its
paradoxical depth and in its shaking and liberating
power. And we can hope only to catch a glimpse of it
in attempting to interpret our story.

Simon the Pharisee is shocked by the attitude of Jesus
to the whore. He receives the answer that the sinners
have greater love than the righteous ones because more
is forgiven them. It is *not* the love of the woman that
brings her forgiveness, but it is the forgiveness she has
received that creates her love. By her love she shows
that much has been forgiven her, while the lack of love
in the Pharisee shows that little has been forgiven him.

Jesus does not forgive the woman, but He declares
that she *is* forgiven. Her state of mind, her ecstasy of
love, show that something has happened to her. And
nothing greater can happen to a human being than that
he is forgiven. For forgiveness means reconciliation in
spite of estrangement; it means reunion in spite of hos-

tility; it means acceptance of those who are unacceptable, and it means reception of those who are rejected.

Forgiveness is unconditional or it is not forgiveness
at all. Forgiveness has the character of "in spite of," but
the righteous ones give it the character of "because."
The sinners, however, cannot do this. They cannot
transform the divine "in spite of" into a human "because." They cannot show facts, because of which they
must be forgiven. God's forgiveness is unconditional.
There is no condition whatsoever in man which would
make him worthy of forgiveness. If forgiveness were
conditional, conditioned by man, no one could be accepted and no one could accept himself. We know that
this is our situation, but we loathe to face it. It is too
great as a gift and too humiliating as a judgment. We
want to contribute something, and if we have learned
that we cannot contribute anything positive, then we
try at least to contribute something negative: the pain
of self-accusation and self-rejection. And then we read
our story and the parable of the Prodigal Son as if they
said: These sinners were forgiven *because* they humil-
iated themselves and confessed that they were unacceptable; because they suffered about their sinful predicament they were made worthy of forgiveness. But
this reading of the story is a misreading, and a dangerous one. If that were the way to our reconciliation with
God, we should have to produce within ourselves the
feeling of unworthiness, the pain of self-rejection, the
anxiety and despair of guilt. There are many Christians
who try this in order to show God and themselves that
they deserve acceptance. They perform an emotional
work of self-punishment after they have realized that

their other good works do not help them. But emotional works do not help either. God's forgiveness is independent of anything we do, even of self-accusation and self-humiliation. If this were not so, how could we ever be certain that our self-rejection is serious enough to deserve forgiveness? Forgiveness creates repentance— this is declared in our story and this is the experience of those who have been forgiven.

The woman in Simon's house comes to Jesus because she *was* forgiven. We do not know exactly what drove her to Jesus. And if we knew, we should certainly find that it was a mixture of motives—spiritual desire as well as natural attraction, the power of the prophet as well as the impression of the human personality. Our story does not psychoanalyze the woman, but neither does it deny human motives which could be psychoanalyzed. Human motives are always ambiguous. The divine forgiveness cuts into these ambiguities, but it does not demand that they become unambiguous before forgiveness can be given. If this were demanded, then forgiveness would never occur. The description of the woman's behavior shows clearly the ambiguities of her motives. Nevertheless, she *is* accepted.

There is no condition for forgiveness. But forgiveness could not come to us if we were not asking for it and receiving it. Forgiveness is an answer, the divine answer, to the question implied in our existence. An answer is answer only for him who has asked, who is aware of the question. This awareness cannot be fabricated. It may be in a hidden place in our souls, covered by many strata of righteousness. It may reach our consciousness in certain moments. Or, day by day, it

may fill our conscious life as well as its unconscious
depths and drive us to the question to which forgiveness is the answer.

In the minds of many people the word "forgiveness"
has connotations which completely contradict the way
Jesus deals with the woman in our story. Many of us
think of solemn acts of pardon, of release from punish-
ment, in other words, of another act of righteousness
by the righteous ones. But genuine forgiveness is participation, reunion overcoming the powers of estrangement. And only because this is so, does forgiveness
make love possible. We cannot love unless we have accepted forgiveness, and the deeper our experience of
forgiveness is, the greater is our love. We cannot love
where we feel rejected, even if the rejection is done in
righteousness. We are hostile towards that to which we
belong and by which we feel judged, even if the judgment is not expressed in words.

As long as we feel rejected by Him, we cannot love
God. He appears to us as an oppressive power, as He
who gives laws according to His pleasure, who judges
according to His commandments, who condemns according to His wrath. But if we have received and
accepted the message that He *is* reconciled, everything
changes. Like a fiery stream His healing power enters
into us; we can affirm Him and with Him our own being
and the others from whom we were estranged, and life
as a whole. Then we realize that His love is the law
of our own being, and that it is the law of reuniting
love. And we understand that what we have experienced as oppression and judgment and wrath is in reality the working of love, which tries to destroy within

us everything which is against love. To love this love is to love God. Theologians have questioned whether man is able to have love towards God; they have replaced love by obedience. But they are refuted by our story. They teach a theology for the righteous ones but not a theology for the sinners. He who is forgiven knows what it means to love God.

And he who loves God is also able to accept life and to love it. This is not the same as to love God. For many pious people in all generations the love of God is the other side of the hatred for life. And there is much hostility towards life in all of us, even in those who have completely surrendered to life. Our hostility towards life is manifested in cynicism and disgust, in bitterness and continuous accusations against life. We feel rejected by life, not so much because of its objective darkness and threats and horrors, but because of our estrangement from its power and meaning. He who is reunited with God, the creative Ground of life, the power of life in everything that lives, is reunited with life. He feels accepted by it and he can love it. He understands that the greater love is, the greater the estrangement which is conquered by it. In metaphorical language I should like to say to those who feel deeply their hostility towards life: Life accepts you; life loves you as a separated part of itself; life wants to reunite you with itself, even when it seems to destroy you.

There is a section of life which is nearer to us than any other and often the most estranged from us: other human beings. We all know about the regions of the human soul in which things look quite different from the way they look on its benevolent surface. In these regions we can find hidden hostilities against those with whom we are in love. We can find envy and torturing doubt about whether we are really accepted by them. And this hostility and anxiety about being rejected by those who are nearest to us can hide itself under the various forms of love: friendship, sensual love, conjugal and family love. But if we have experienced ultimate acceptance this anxiety is conquered, though not re- moved. We can love without being sure of the answer- ing love of the other one. For we know that he himself is longing for our acceptance as we are longing for his, and that in the light of ultimate acceptance we are united.

He who is accepted ultimately can also accept him- self. Being forgiven and being able to accept oneself are one and the same thing. No one can accept himself who does not feel that he is accepted by the power of acceptance which is greater than he, greater than his friends and counselors and psychological helpers. They may point to the power of acceptance, and it is the function of the minister to do so. But he and the others also need the power of acceptance which is greater than they. The woman in our story could never have overcome her disgust at her own being without finding this power working through Jesus, who told her with authority, "You *are* forgiven." Thus, she experienced, at least in *one* ecstatic moment of her life, the power which reunited her with herself and gave her the pos- sibility of loving even her own destiny.

This happened to her in one great moment. And in this she is no exception. Decisive spiritual experiences have the character of a break-through. In the midst of our futile attempts to make ourselves worthy, in our despair about the inescapable failure of these attempts, we are suddenly grasped by the certainty that we are forgiven, and the fire of love begins to burn. That is the greatest experience anyone can have. It may not happen often, but when it does happen, it decides and transforms everything.

And now let us look once more at those whom we have described as the righteous ones. They are really righteous, but since little is forgiven them, they love little. And this is their unrighteousness. It does not lie on the moral level, just as the unrighteousness of Job did not lie on the moral level where his friends sought for it in vain. It lies on the level of the encounter with ultimate reality, with the God who vindicates Job's righteousness against the attacks of his friends, with the God who defends Himself against the attacks of Job and his ultimate unrighteousness. The righteousness of the righteous ones is hard and self-assured. They, too, want forgiveness, but they believe that they do not need much of it. And so their righteous actions are warmed by very little love. They could not have helped the woman in our story, and they cannot help us, even if we admire them. Why do children turn from their righteous parents and husbands from their righteous wives, and vice versa? Why do Christians turn away from their righteous pastors? Why do people turn away from righteous neighborhoods? Why do many turn away from righteous Christianity and from the Jesus it paints and the God it proclaims? Why do they turn to those who are not considered to be the righteous ones? Often, certainly, it is because they want to escape judgment.

But more often it is because they seek a love which is rooted in forgiveness, and this the righteous ones cannot give. Many of those to whom they turn cannot give it either. Jesus gave it to the woman who was utterly unacceptable. The Church would be more the Church of Christ than it is now if it did the same, if it joined Jesus and not Simon in its encounter with those who are rightly judged unacceptable. Each of us who strives for righteousness would be more Christian if more were forgiven him, if he loved more and if he could better resist the temptation to present himself as acceptable to God by his own righteousness.

2

THE NEW BEING

For neither circumcision counts for anything nor uncircumcision, but a new creation.

GALATIANS 6:15.

IF I WERE ASKED TO SUM UP THE Christian message for our time in two words, I would say with Paul: It is the message of a "New Creation." We have read something of the New Creation in Paul's second letter to the Corinthians. Let me repeat one of his sentences in the words of an exact translation: "If anyone is in union with Christ he is a new being; the old state of things has passed away; there is a new state of things." Christianity is the message of the New Creation, the New Being, the New Reality which has appeared with the appearance of Jesus who for this reason, and just for this reason, is called the Christ. For the Christ, the Messiah, the selected and anointed one is He who brings the new state of things.

We all live in the old state of things, and the question asked of us by our text is whether we *also* participate in the new state of things. We belong to the Old Creation, and the demand made upon us by Christianity is that we *also* participate in the New Creation. We have known ourselves in our old being, and we

15

shall ask ourselves in this hour whether we also have
experienced something of a New Being in ourselves.

What is this New Being? Paul answers first by saying
what it is *not*. It is neither circumcision, nor uncircumcision, he says. For Paul and for the readers of his letter this meant something very definite. It meant that
neither to be a Jew nor to be a pagan is ultimately important; that only one thing counts, namely, the union
with Him in whom the New Reality is present. Circumcision or uncircumcision—what does that mean for *us*?
It can also mean something very definite, but at the
same time something very universal. It means that no
religion as such produces the New Being. Circumcision
is a religious rite, observed by the Jews; sacrifices are
religious rites, observed by the pagans; baptism is a
religious rite, observed by the Christians. All these rites
do not matter—only a New Creation. And since these
rites stand, in the words of Paul, for the whole religion
to which they belong, we can say: No religion matters—
only a new state of things. Let us think about this strik-
ing assertion of Paul. What it says first is that Christianity is more than a religion; it is the message of a New
Creation. Christianity as a religion is not important—
it is like circumcision or like uncircumcision: no more,
no less! Are we able even to imagine the consequences
of the apostolic pronouncement for our situation? Christianity in the present world encounters several forms
of circumcision and uncircumcision. Circumcision can
stand today for everything called religion, uncircumcision for everything called secular, but making half-
religious claims. There are the great religions beside
Christianity, Hinduism, Buddhism, Islam and the rem-

nants of classical Judaism; they have their myths and
their rites—so to speak their "circumcision"—which gives
each of them their distinction. There are the secular
movements: Fascism and Communism, Secular Hu-
manism, and Ethical Idealism. They try to avoid myths
and rites; they represent, so to speak, uncircumcision.
Nevertheless, they also claim ultimate truth and demand complete devotion. How shall Christianity face
them? Shall Christianity tell them: Come to us, we
are a better religion, our kind of circumcision or uncircumcision is higher than yours? Shall we praise
Christianity, our way of life, the religious as well as the
secular? Shall we make of the Christian message a success story, and tell them, like advertisers: try it with us,
and you will see how important Christianity is for everybody? Some missionaries and some ministers and some
Christian laymen use these methods. They show a total
misunderstanding of Christianity. The apostle who was
a missionary and a minister and a layman all at once
says something different. He says: No particular religion matters, neither ours nor yours. But I want to tell
you that something has happened that matters, something that judges you and me, your religion and my
religion. A New Creation has occurred, a New Being
has appeared; and we are all asked to participate in it.
And so we should say to the pagans and Jews wherever
we meet them: Don't compare your religion and our
religion, your rites and our rites, your prophets and our
prophets, your priests and our priests, the pious amongst
you, and the pious amongst us. All this is of no avail!
And above all don't think that we want to convert you
to English or American Christianity, to the religion of

the Western World. We do not want to convert you to us, not even to the best of us. This would be of no avail. We want only to show you something we have seen and to tell you something we have heard: That in the midst of the old creation there is a New Creation, and that this New Creation is manifest in Jesus who is called the Christ.

And when we meet Fascists and Communists, Scientific Humanists and Ethical Idealists, we should say to them: Don't boast too much that you have no rites and myths, that you are free from superstitions, that you are perfectly reasonable, uncircumcised in every sense. In the first place, you also have your rites and myths, your bit of circumcision; they are even very important to you. But if you were completely free from them you would have no reason to point to your *un*circumcision. It is of no avail. Don't think that we want to convert you away from your secular state to a religious state, that we want to make you religious and members of a very high religion, the Christian, and of a very great denomination within it, namely, our own. This would be of no avail. We want only to communicate to you an experience we have had that here and there in the world and now and then in ourselves is a New Creation, usually hidden, but sometimes manifest, and certainly manifest in Jesus who is called the Christ.

This is the way we should speak to all those outside the Christian realm, whether they are religious or secular. And we should not be too worried about the Christian religion, about the state of the Churches, about membership and doctrines, about institutions and ministers, about sermons and sacraments. This is circumcision; and the lack of it, the secularization which today is spreading all over the world is uncircumcision. Both are nothing, of no importance, if the ultimate question is asked, the question of a New Reality. *This* question, however, is of infinite importance. We should worry more about it than about anything else between heaven and earth. The New Creation—this is our ultimate concern; this should be our infinite passion—the infinite passion of every human being. This matters; this alone matters ultimately. In comparison with it everything else, even religion or non-religion, even Christianity or non-Christianity, matters very little—and ultimately nothing.

And now let me boast for a moment about the fact that we are Christians and let us become fools by boasting, as Paul called himself when he started boasting. It is the greatness of Christianity that it can see how small it is. The importance of being a Christian is that we can stand the insight that it is of no importance. It is the spiritual power of religion that he who is religious can fearlessly look at the vanity of religion. It is the maturest fruit of Christian understanding to understand that Christianity, as such, is of no avail. This is boasting, not personal boasting, but boasting about Christianity. As boasting it is foolishness. But as boasting about the fact that there is nothing to boast about, it is wisdom and maturity. Having as having not—this is the right attitude toward everything great and wonderful in life, even religion and Christianity. But it is not the right attitude toward the New Creation. Toward it the right attitude is passionate and infinite longing.

And now we ask again: What is this New Being? The

New Being is not something that simply takes the place of the Old Being. But it is a renewal of the Old which has been corrupted, distorted, split and almost destroyed. But not wholly destroyed. Salvation does not destroy creation; but it transforms the Old Creation into a New one. Therefore we can speak of the New in terms of a *re*-newal: The threefold *"re,"* namely, *re*-conciliation, *re*-union, *re*-surrection.

In his letter, Paul combines New Creation with reconciliation. The message of reconciliation is: *Be* reconciled to God. Cease to be hostile to Him, for He is never hostile to you. The message of reconciliation is not that God needs to be reconciled. How could He be? Since He is the source and power of reconciliation, who could reconcile Him? Pagans and Jews and Christians— all of us have tried and are trying to reconcile Him by rites and sacraments, by prayers and services, by moral behavior and works of charity. But if we try this, if we try to give something to Him, to show good deeds which may appease Him, we fail. It is never enough; we never can satisfy Him because there is an infinite demand upon us. And since we cannot appease Him, we grow hostile toward Him. Have you ever noticed how much hostility against God dwells in the depths of the good and honest people, in those who excel in works of charity, in piety and religious zeal? This cannot be otherwise; for one is hostile, consciously or unconsciously, toward those by whom one feels rejected. Everybody is in this predicament, whether he calls that which rejects him "God," or "nature," or "destiny," or "social conditions." Everybody carries a hostility toward the existence into which he has been thrown, toward the hidden powers which determine his life and that of the universe, toward that which makes him guilty and that threatens him with destruction because he has become guilty. We all feel rejected and hostile toward what has rejected us. We all try to appease it and in failing, we become more hostile. This happens often unnoticed by ourselves. But there are two symptoms which we hardly can avoid noticing: The hostility against ourselves and the hostility against others. One speaks so often of pride and arrogance and self-certainty and complacency in people. But this is, in most cases, the superficial level of their being. Below this, in a deeper level, there is self-rejection, disgust, and even hatred of one's self. Be reconciled to God; that means at the same time, be reconciled to ourselves. But we are not; we try to appease ourselves. We try to make ourselves more acceptable to our own judgment and, when we fail, we grow more hostile toward ourselves. And he who feels rejected by God and who rejects himself feels also rejected by the others. As he grows hostile toward destiny and hostile toward himself, he also grows hostile toward other men. If we are often horrified by the unconscious or conscious hostility people betray toward us or about our own hostility toward people whom we believe we love, let us not forget: They feel rejected by us; we feel rejected by them. They tried hard to make themselves acceptable to us, and they failed. We tried hard to make ourselves acceptable to them, and we failed. And their and our hostility grew. Be reconciled with God—that means, at the same time, be reconciled with the others! But it does *not* mean try to reconcile the others, as it does not mean try to reconcile yourselves.

Try to reconcile God. You will fail. This is the message: A new reality has appeared in which you *are* reconciled. To enter the New Being we do not need to show anything. We must only be open to be grasped by it, although we have nothing to show.

Being reconciled—that is the first mark of the New Reality. And being reunited is its second mark. Reconciliation makes reunion possible. The New Creation is the reality in which the separated is reunited. The New Being is manifest in the Christ because in Him the separation never overcame the unity between Him and God, between Him and mankind, between Him and Himself. This gives His picture in the Gospels its overwhelming and inexhaustible power. In Him we look at a human life that maintained the union in spite of everything that drove Him into separation. He represents and mediates the power of the New Being because He represents and mediates the power of an undisrupted union. Where the New Reality appears, one feels united with God, the ground and meaning of one's existence. One has what has been called the love of one's destiny, and what, today, we might call the courage to take upon ourselves our own anxiety. Then one has the astonishing experience of feeling reunited with one's self, not in pride and false self-satisfaction, but in a deep self-acceptance. One accepts one's self as something which is eternally important, eternally loved, eternally accepted. The disgust at one's self, the hatred of one's self has disappeared. There is a center, a direction, a meaning for life. All healing—bodily and mental —creates this reunion of one's self with one's self. Where there is real healing, *there* is the New Being, the New Creation. But real healing is not where only a part of body or mind is reunited with the whole, but where the whole itself, our whole being, our whole personality is united with itself. The New Creation is healing creation because it creates reunion with oneself. And it creates reunion with the others. Nothing is more distinctive of the Old Being than the separation of man from man. Nothing is more passionately demanded than social healing, than the New Being within history and human relationships. Religion and Christianity are under strong accusation that they have not brought reunion into human history. Who could deny the truth of this challenge. Nevertheless, mankind still lives; and it could not live any more if the power of separation had not been permanently conquered by the power of reunion, of healing, of the New Creation. Where one is grasped by a human face as human, although one has to overcome personal distaste, or racial strangeness, or national conflicts, or the differences of sex, of age, of beauty, of strength, of knowledge, and all the other innumerable causes of separation—*there* New Creation happens! Mankind lives because this happens again and again. And if the Church which is the assembly of God has an ultimate significance, this is its significance: That here the reunion of man to man is pronounced and confessed and realized, even if in fragments and weaknesses and distortions. The Church is the place where the reunion of man with man is an actual event, though the Church of God is permanently betrayed by the Christian churches. But, although betrayed and expelled, the New Creation saves and preserves that by which it is betrayed and expelled: churches, mankind and history.

The Church, like all its members, relapses from the New into the Old Being. Therefore, the third mark of the New Creation is re-surrection. The word "resurrection" has for many people the connotation of dead bodies leaving their graves or other fanciful images. But resurrection means the victory of the New state of things, the New Being born out of the death of the Old. Resurrection is not an event that might happen in some remote future, but it is the power of the New Being to create life out of death, here and now, today and tomorrow. Where there is a New Being, *there* is resurrection, namely, the creation into eternity out of every moment of time. The Old Being has the mark of disintegration and death. The New Being puts a new mark over the old one. Out of disintegration and death something is born of eternal significance. That which is immersed in dissolution emerges in a New Creation. Resurrection happens *now*, or it does not happen at all. It happens in us and around us, in soul and history, in nature and universe.

Reconciliation, reunion, resurrection—this is the New Creation, the New Being, the New state of things. Do we participate in it? The message of Christianity is not Christianity, but a New Reality. A New state of things has appeared, it still appears; it is hidden and visible, it is there and it is here. Accept it, enter into it, let it grasp you.

3

THE POWER OF LOVE

*When the Son of man comes in his glory, and all
the angels with him, then he will sit on his glorious
throne. Before him will be gathered all the nations,
and he will separate them from one another as a
shepherd separates the sheep from the goats, and he
will place the sheep at his right hand, but the goats
at the left. Then the King will say to those at his
right hand, "Come, O blessed of my Father, inherit
the kingdom prepared for you from the foundation
of the world; for I was hungry and you gave me food,
I was thirsty and you gave me drink, I was a stranger
and you welcomed me, I was naked and you clothed
me, I was sick and you visited me, I was in prison
and you came to me." Then the righteous will answer him, "Lord, when did we see thee hungry and
feed thee, or thirsty and give thee drink? And when
did we see thee a stranger and welcome thee, or
naked and clothe thee? And when did we see thee
sick or in prison and visit thee?" And the King will
answer them, "Truly, I say to you, as you did it to
one of these my brethren, you did it to me."*

MATTHEW 25:31-40.

So we know and believe the love God has for us.

God is love, and he who abides in love abides in God, and God abides in him.

I JOHN 4:16.

A new commandment I give to you, that you love one another; even as I have loved you, that you also love one another. By this all men will know that you are my disciples, if you have love for one another.

JOHN 13:34-35.

AFTER TWO THOUSAND YEARS ARE WE still able to realize what it means to say, "God *is* Love"? The writer of the First Epistle of John certainly knew what he wrote, for he drew the consequences: "He who abides in love abides in God, and God abides in him." God's abiding in us, making us His dwelling place, is the same thing as our abiding in love, as our having love as the sphere of our habitation. God and love are not two realities; they are one. God's Being is the being of love and God's infinite power of Being is the infinite power of love. Therefore, he who professes devotion to God *may* abide in God if he abides in love, or he may not abide in God if he does not abide in love. And he who does not speak of God may abide in Him if he is abiding in love. And since the manifestation of God as love is His manifestation in Jesus the Christ, Jesus can say that many of those who do not know Him, belong to Him, and that many of those who confess their allegiance to Him do not belong to Him. The criterion, the only ultimate criterion, is love. For God is love, and the divine love is triumphantly manifest in Christ the Crucified.

Let me tell you the story of a woman who died a few years ago and whose life was spent abiding in love, although she rarely, if ever, used the name of God, and though she would have been surprised had someone told her that she belonged to Him who judges all men, because He is love and love is the only criterion of His judgment.

Her name was Elsa Brandström, the daughter of a former Swedish ambassador to Russia. But her name in the mouths and hearts of hundreds of thousands of prisoners of war during the First World War was the Angel of Siberia. She was an irrefutable, living witness to the truth that love is the ultimate power of Being, even in a century which belongs to the darkest, most destructive and cruel of all centuries since the dawn of mankind.

At the beginning of the First World War, when Elsa Brandström was twenty-four years old, she looked out of the window of the Swedish Embassy in what was then St. Petersburg and saw the German prisoners of war being driven through the streets on their way to Siberia. From that moment on she could no longer endure the splendor of the diplomatic life of which, up to then, she had been a beautiful and vigorous center. She became a nurse and began visiting the prison camps. There she saw unspeakable horrors and she, a girl of twenty-four, began, almost alone, the fight of love against cruelty, and she prevailed. She had to fight against the resistance and suspicion of the authorities and she prevailed. She had to fight against the brutality and lawlessness of the prison guards and she prevailed. She had to fight against cold, hunger, dirt and illness, against the conditions of an undeveloped country and a destructive war, and she prevailed. Love gave her wisdom with innocence, and daring with foresight. And whenever she appeared despair was conquered and sorrow healed. She visited the hungry and gave them food. She saw the thirsty and gave them to drink. She welcomed the strangers, clothed the naked and strengthened the sick. She herself fell ill and was imprisoned, but God was abiding in her. The irresistible power of love was with her.

And she never ceased to be driven by this power. After the war she initiated a great work for the orphans of German and Russian prisoners of war. The sight of her among these children whose sole ever-shining sun she was, must have been a decisive religious impression for many people. With the coming of the Nazis, she and her husband were forced to leave Germany and come to this country. Here she became the helper of innumerable European refugees, and for ten years I was able personally to observe the creative genius of her love. We never had a theological conversation. It was unnecessary. She made God transparent in every moment. For God, who is love, was abiding in her and she in Him. She aroused the love of millions towards herself and towards that for which she was transparent—the God who is love. On her deathbed she received a delegate from the king and people of Sweden, representing innumerable people all over Europe, assuring her that she would never be forgotten by those to whom she had given back the meaning of their lives.

It is a rare gift to meet a human being in whom love
—and this means God—is so overwhelmingly manifest.
It undercuts theological arrogance as well as pious isolation. It is more than justice and it is greater than
faith and hope. It is the presence of God Himself. For
God is love. And in every moment of genuine love we
are dwelling in God and God in us.

4

THE GOLDEN RULE

*God is love, and he who abides in love abides in
God and God abides in him. No man has ever seen
God. If we love one another, God abides in us and
his love is perfected in us . . .*

I JOHN 4:16, 12.

*So whatever you wish that men would do to you,
do so to them; for this is the law and the prophets.*

MATTHEW 7:12.

RECENTLY I HAVE HAD TO THINK ABOUT
the relation of love to justice. And it occurred to me
that among the words of Jesus there is a statement of
what is called the "Golden Rule." The Golden Rule
was well known to Jews and Greeks, although mostly
in a negative form: What you do NOT want that men
should do to you, do NOT so to them. Certainly, the
positive form is richer in meaning and nearer to love,
but it is not love. It is calculating justice. How, then,
is it related to love? How does it fit the message of
the kingdom of God and the justice of the kingdom as
expressed in the Sermon on the Mount where the
Golden Rule appears?

Let us think of an ordinary day in our life and of

occasions for the application of the Golden Rule. We meet each other in the morning, we expect a friendly face or word and we are ready to give it although our minds are full of anxious anticipation of the burdens of the day. Somebody wants a part of our limited time, we give it, having asked somebody else to give us a part of his time. We need help and we give it if we are asked, although it includes sacrifice. We are frank with others, expecting that they will be frank with us even if it hurts. We are fair to those who fight against us, expecting fairness from them. We participate in the sorrows of our neighbors, certain that they will participate in ours. All this can happen in one day. All this is Golden Rule. And if somebody has violated this rule, consciously or unconsciously, we are willing to forgive as we hope to be forgiven. It is not astonishing that for many people the Golden Rule is considered as the real content of Christianity. It is not surprising that in the name of the Golden Rule criticism is suppressed, independent action discouraged, serious problems avoided. It is even understandable that statesmen ask other nations to behave towards their own nation according to the Golden Rule. And does not Jesus Himself say that the Golden Rule is the law and the prophets?

But we know that this is not the answer of the New Testament. The great commandment as Jesus repeats it and the descriptions of love in Paul and John's tremendous assertion that God *is* love, infinitely transcend the Golden Rule. It must be transcended, for it does not tell us what we *should* wish that men would do to us. We wish to have freedom from heavy duties. We are ready to give the same freedom to others. But some-

one who loves us refuses to give it to us, and he himself
refuses to ask us for it. And if he did, we should refuse
to give it to him because it would reduce our growth
and violate the law of love. We wish to receive a fortune
which makes us secure and independent. We would be
ready to give a fortune to a friend who asks us for it, if
we had it. But in both cases love would be violated. For
the gift would ruin us and him. We want to be forgiven
and we are ready to do the same. But perhaps it is in
both cases an escape from the seriousness of a personal
problem, and therefore against love.

The measure of what we shall do to men cannot be
our wishes about what they shall do to us. For our
wishes express not only our right but also our wrong,
and our foolishness more than our wisdom. This is the
limit of the Golden Rule. This is the limit of calculating justice. Only for him who knows what he *should*
wish and who actually wishes it, is the Golden Rule
ultimately valid. Only love can transform calculating
justice into creative justice. Love makes justice just.
Justice without love is always injustice because it does
not do justice to the other one, nor to oneself, nor to
the situation in which we meet. For the other one and
I and we together in this moment in this place are a
unique, unrepeatable occasion, calling for a unique
unrepeatable act of uniting love. If this call is not heard
by listening love, if it is not obeyed by the creative
genius of love, injustice is done. And this is true even
of oneself. He who loves listens to the call of his own
innermost center and obeys this call and does justice
to his own being.

For love does not remove, it establishes justice. It

does not add something to what justice does but it shows justice what to do. It makes the Golden Rule possible. For we do not speak for a love which swallows justice. This would result in chaos and extinction. But we speak for a love in which justice is the form and structure of love. We speak for a love which respects the claim of the other one to be acknowledged as what he is, and the claim of ourselves to be acknowledged as what we are, above all as persons. Only distorted love, which is a cover for hostility or self-disgust, denies that which love unites. Love makes justice just. The divine love is justifying love accepting and fulfilling him who, according to calculating justice, must be rejected. The justification of him who is unjust is the fulfillment of God's creative justice, and of His reuniting love.

5

ON HEALING (Part I)

And he called to him his twelve disciples and gave them authority over unclean spirits, to cast them out, and to heal every disease and every infirmity.

MATTHEW 10:1.

RECENTLY I SPENT THREE MONTHS IN Germany and what I saw was a sick people, sick as a whole and sick as individuals. Their faces are shaped by burdens too heavy to be carried, by sorrows too deep to be forgotten. And what their faces expressed, their words confirmed: Tales of horror, stories of pain and despair, anxieties dwelling in their blood, confusions and self-contradictions disturbing their minds. And if you look deeper into them you find guilt-feeling, sometimes expressed, mostly repressed. For it hides itself under passionate denials of guilt, under self-excuse and accusations of others, under a mixture of hostility and humility, of self-pity and self-hate. The nation is split externally by the split between East and West which divides all mankind politically and spiritually. And the nation is split internally. Old hostilities are smoldering, new hostilities are growing, and there is no peace. A sick nation.

But within this nation I found people who were healthy, not because the sickness was not written in their faces also. But something else was in them, a healing power, making them whole in spite of their disruption, making them serene in spite of their sorrow, making them examples for all of us, examples of what could and should happen to us!

To us? But are we not a healthy nation? That certainly is what you believe when you return from Germany and Europe to this country! The faces of most people are shaped by smiles and not by tears. There is benevolence towards each other and even towards enemies. People here are willing to admit their shortcomings such as discrimination, exploitation, destructive competition. They are used to acting spontaneously and not under compulsions imposed on them by tyrants or conquerors, or what is even more difficult, imposed on them by newspapers, radios and public opinion polls, these tyrants of modern democracy. A healthy nation!

But we read that in this nation almost 40 per cent of all those young men who are rejected by the Armed Services are unacceptable because of mental disturbances and maladjustments. And we hear that of all illnesses mental illness is by far the most widespread in this country. What does this mean? It is a symptom of serious danger for our health. There may be something in the structure of our institutions which produces illness in more and more people. It may, for instance, be that the unlimited, ruthless competition which deprives everybody of a feeling of security, makes many in our healthy nation sick; not only those who are unsuccessful in competition, but also those who are most successful. And so something surprising occurs: We have fought victoriously against many forms of bodily sickness. We have discovered drugs with an almost miraculous power. The average length of our lives has been stretched beyond any former expectation. But many in our nation cannot stand this health. They want sickness as a refuge into which they can escape from the harshness of an insecure life. And since the medical care has made it more difficult to escape into bodily illness, they choose *mental* illness. But does not everybody dislike sickness, the pain, the discomfort and the danger connected with it? Of course, we dislike our sickness with some parts of our souls; but we like it with some other parts, mostly unconsciously, sometimes even consciously. But nobody can be healed especially of mental disorders and diseases who does not want it with his whole heart. And this is why they have become almost an epidemic in this country. People are fleeing into a situation where others must take care of them, where they exercise power through weakness or where they create an imaginary world in which it is nice to live as long as real life does not touch them. Don't underestimate this temptation. The basic insecurity of human existence and the driving anxiety connected with it are felt everywhere and by everyone. It is human heritage and it is increased immensely by our present world, even in this country full of vigor and health.

As in ours, so in the period of Jesus much talk was going on of sickness and healing. Jews and Greeks wrote about it. People felt that they lived in a sick period; they called it "*this* world-period" and they described it in a way which is very similar to the way in which we describe it today. They saw not only the bodily infirmity of all of us, the innumerable bodily diseases in the masses of the people, they also saw the destructive powers possessing the minds of many. They called the mentally ill the possessed or the demoniacs and they tried to expel the evil spirits. They also knew that nations can be sick and that the diseases of social classes infect every individual in it. They looked even beyond the boundary lines of mankind into nature and spoke in visionary ecstasy about this earth becoming old and sick just as we did when we were under the first shock of the atomic power of self-destruction. Out of this knowledge of a sick period the question of a new period, a reality of health and wholeness was asked. Salvation and a savior were expected. But salvation is healing. And the savior is the healer. Therefore, Jesus answers the anxious question of the Baptist about whether He is the Savior, by pointing to His healing power. This is what He says: "If I am able to heal the deaf and the blind, if I am able to liberate the mentally sick, then a new reality has come upon you!" There are many healing stories in the Gospels, a stumbling block for scholars and preachers and teachers, because they take them as miracle stories of the past instead of taking them as healing stories of the present. For this they are. They show the human situation, the relation between bodily and mental disease, between sickness and guilt, between the desire of being healed and the fear of being healed. It is astonishing how many of our profoundest modern insights into human nature are anticipated in these stories: They know that becoming healthy means becoming whole, reunited, in one's bodily and psychic functions. They know that the mentally sick are afraid of the process of healing, because it throws them out of the limited but safe house of their neurotic self-seclusion, they know that the process of mental healing is a difficult and painful one, accompanied by convulsions of body and soul. They tell of the relation of guilt and disease, of the way in which unsolved conflicts of our conscience drive us to those cleavages of body and soul which we call sickness. We are told how Jesus, knowing this, pronounces to the paralytic first the forgiveness of his sins and then his regained health. The man lived in an inner struggle with himself, with his feeling of guilt. Out of this conflict his illness had grown; and now when Jesus forgives him, he feels reconciled with himself and the world; he becomes whole and healthy. There is little in our recent psychology of depth that surpasses these insights in truth and depth. These stories also describe the attitude which makes healing possible. They call it faith. Faith here, of course, does not mean the belief in assertions for which there is no evidence. It never meant that in genuine religion, and it never should be abused in this sense. But faith means being grasped by a power that is greater than we are, a power that shakes us and turns us, and transforms us and heals us. Surrender to this power is faith. The people whom Jesus could heal and can heal are those who did and do this self-surrender to the healing power in Him. They surrendered their persons, split, contradicting themselves, disgusted and despairing about themselves, hateful of themselves and therefore hostile towards everybody else; afraid of life, burdened with guilt feelings, accusing and excusing themselves, fleeing from others into loneliness, fleeing from themselves to others, trying finally to escape from the threats of existence into the painful and deceptive safety of mental and bodily disease. As such beings they surrendered to Jesus and this surrender is what we call faith. But he did not keep them, as a good helper should never do. He gave them back to themselves, as new creatures, healed and whole. And when He died He left a group of people who, in spite of much anxiety and discord and weakness and guilt, had the certitude that they were healed, and that the healing power amongst them was great enough to conquer individuals and nations all over the world. We belong to these people, if we are grasped by the new reality which has appeared in Him. We *have* His healing power ourselves.

Jesus was called a physician, and it is the physician for whom we ask first when we are looking for health. And this is good. For, as all generations knew, there is healing power in nature. And much healing is possible if this power is wisely used and skillfully aided. Those who despise this aid and rely on the power of their will ignore both the destructive might and the constructive friendliness of nature. They do not know that our body contains not only forces of discord between its elements but also forces of concord. The great physician is he who does not easily cut off parts and does not easily suppress the one function in favor of the other, but he who strengthens the whole so that within the unity of the body the struggling elements can be reconciled. And this is possible even if deep traces of former struggles in our body remain as long as we live.

The physician can help, he can keep us alive, but can he make us whole? Can he give us salvation? Certainly not, if discord, cleavage, restlessness rule our mental life, if there is no unity and therefore no freedom in our soul, if we are possessed by compulsions and fantasies, by disordered anxiety and disordered aggression, if mental disorder or disease are threatening or have conquered us. Then if we want to be healed, we ask for the help of friends or counselors or analysts or psychiatrists. And they, if they know what to do, try to aid the healing powers of our soul. They do not appeal to our will power; they do not ask for removal or suppression of any trend, but they work for reconciliation, reconciliation of the struggling forces of our soul. They accept us as we are and make it possible for us to look at ourselves honestly and with clarity, to realize the strange mechanisms under which we are suffering and to dissolve them, reconciling the genuine forces of our soul with each other and making us free for thought and action.

The counselor and psychiatrist can *help;* he can liberate us, but can he make us whole? Can he give us salvation? Certainly not if we are not able to use our freedom and if we are conquered by the tragic conflicts of our existence. None of us is isolated. We belong to our past, to our families, classes, groups, nations, cultures. And in all of them health and illness are fighting with each other. How can we be whole if the culture is split within itself, if every value is denied by another one, if every truth is questioned, if every decision is good and bad at the same time? How can we be whole if the institutions in which we live create temptations, conflicts, catastrophes too heavy for each of us? How can we be whole if we are connected, often intimately connected with people who are in discord with themselves, in hostility against us, or if we have to live with people, individuals, groups, nations who are irreconciled and sick? This is the situation of all of us, and this situation reacts on our personal life, disrupts the concord we may have reached. The reconciliation in our souls and often even in our bodies breaks down in the encounter with reality. Who heals reality? Who brings us a new reality? Who reconciles the conflicting forces of our whole existence? We look at those who are most responsible for our institutions, for our historical reality, the leaders, the statesmen, the wise administrators, the educated, the good people, the revolutionary masses. There are healing powers in all of them, otherwise there would be no more history. And it is understandable that in the period of Jesus just rulers were called saviors and healers. They can maintain human life on earth; but can they make us whole, can they bring us salvation?

They cannot because they themselves need wholeness and are longing for salvation. Who heals the healer? There is no answer to this in the old reality. Everybody and every institution are infected, the healer and the healed. Only a new reality can make us whole, breaking into the old one, reconciling it with itself. It is the humanly incredible, ecstatic, often defeated, but never conquered faith of Christianity that this new reality which was always at work in history, has appeared in fullness and power in Jesus, the Christ, the Healer and Savior. This is said of Him because He alone does not give another law for thought or action, because He does not cut off anything or suppress anything that belongs to life, but because He is the reality of reconciliation, because in Him a new reality has come upon us in which we and our whole existence are accepted and reunited. We know, even when we confess this faith, that the old reality of conflict and disease has not disappeared. Our bodies ail and die, our souls are restless, our world is a battlefield of individuals and groups. But the new reality cannot be thrown out. We live from it, even if we do not know it. For it is the power of reconciliation whose work is wholeness and whose name is love.

ON HEALING (Part II)

The Lord healeth the broken in heart, and bindeth up their wounds—Bless the Lord, O my soul . . . who healeth all thy diseases, who redeemeth thy life from destruction.

PSALM 147:3; 103:2, 3, 4.

HOW DO WE PAINT JESUS THE CHRIST? It does not matter whether He is painted in lines and colors, as the great Christian painters in all periods have done or whether we paint Him in sermons, as the Christian preachers have done Sunday after Sunday, or whether we paint Him in learned books, in Biblical or systematic theology, or whether we paint Him in

our hearts, in devotion, imagination and love. In each
case we must answer the question: How do we paint
Jesus the Christ? The stories in the Gospel of Matthew
contribute to the answer; they add a color, an expression, a trait of great intensity, they paint Him as the
healer: It is astonishing that this color, this vivid expression of His nature, this powerful trait of His character, has more and more been lost in our time. The
grayish colors of a moral teacher, the tense expression
of a social reformer, the soft traits of a suffering servant
have prevailed, at least amongst our painters and theologians and life-of-Jesus novelists; perhaps not so much
in the hearts of the people who need somebody to heal
them.

The gospels, certainly, are not responsible for this dis-
appearance of power in the picture of Jesus. They
abound in stories of healing; but *we* are responsible,
ministers, laymen, theologians, who forgot that "Savior"
means "healer," he who makes whole and sane what is
broken and insane, in body and mind. The woman who
encountered Him was made whole, the demoniac who
met Him was liberated from his mental cleavage. Those
who are disrupted, split, disintegrated, are healed by
Him. And because this is so, because this power has
appeared on earth, the Kingdom of God has come upon
us; this is the answer Jesus gives to the Pharisees when
they discuss His power of healing the mentally possessed; this is the answer He gives to the Baptist to
overcome his doubts; this is the order He gives to His
disciples when He sends them to the towns of Israel.
"And as ye go, preach, saying, the kingdom of God is
at hand. Heal the sick, raise the dead, cleanse the lepers,

cast out demons." That is what they shall do and for *this* He gives them authority and power; for in Him the kingdom of God has appeared, and its nature is salvation, healing of that which is ill, making whole what is broken.

Are we still able to experience this power? I do not speak of theological inhibitions about the acceptance of such a picture of the Christ. They do not weigh very heavily. Of course we were worried about miracle-stories for many decades; today we know what the New Testament always knew—that miracles are signs pointing to the presence of a divine power in nature and history, and that they are in no way negations of natural laws. Of course, we were and we are worried about the abuse of religious healing for commercial and other selfish purposes or about its distortion into magic and superstition. But abuses occur when the right use is lacking and superstitions arise when faith has become weak. All these are not serious problems; good theology and good practice can solve them.

But the serious problem is, as always, the problem of our own existence. Are we healed, have we received healing forces, here and there from the power of the picture of Jesus as the Savior? Are we grasped by this power? Is it strong enough to overcome our neurotic trends, the rebellion of unconscious strivings, the split in our conscious being, the diseases which disintegrate our minds and destroy our bodies at the same time? Have we overcome in moments of grace the torturing anxiety in the depth of our hearts, the restlessness which never ceases moving and whipping us, the unordered desires and the hidden repressions which return as poisonous hate, the hostility against ourselves and others, against life itself, the hidden will to death? Have we experienced now and then in moments of grace that we are made whole, that destructive spirits have left us, that psychic compulsions are dissolved, that tyrannical mechanisms in our soul are replaced by freedom; that despair, this most dangerous of all splits, this real sickness unto death, is healed and we are saved from self-destruction? Has this happened to us under the power of the picture of Jesus as the Savior? This is the real problem, the true Christological problem (theologically speaking), the question of life and death (humanly speaking), for every Christian and of Christendom of today. Do we go to the physicians alone, or to the psychotherapists alone or to the counsellors alone in order to be healed? Sometimes, of course, we should go to them, but do we also go to or—more precisely— do we also receive the healing power in the picture of Jesus the Christ who is called the Savior? This is the question before us, and this question is answered by those who can tell us that they have experienced His healing power, that the New Being *has* grasped their bodies and their soul, that they *have* become whole and sane again, that salvation *has* come upon them. Not always, of course, but in those moments which are moments of grace and in which they anticipated the perfect wholeness, the wholeness of God being in all. Can we join this answer?

6

HOLY WASTE

And while he was at Bethany in the house of Simon the leper, as he sat at table, a woman came with an alabaster jar of ointment of pure nard, very costly, and she broke the jar and poured it over his head. But there were some who said to themselves indignantly, "Why was the ointment thus wasted? For this ointment might have been sold for more than three hundred denarii, and given to the poor." And they reproached her. But Jesus said, "Let her alone; why do you trouble her? She has done a beautiful thing to me. For you always have the poor with you, and whenever you will, you can do good to them; but you will not always have me. She has done what she could; she has anointed my body beforehand for burying. And truly, I say to you, wherever the gospel is preached in the whole world, what she has done will be told in memory of her."

MARK 14:3-9.

WHAT HAS SHE DONE? SHE HAS GIVEN an example of a waste, which, as Jesus says, is a beautiful thing. It is, so to speak, a holy waste, a waste growing out of the abundance of the heart. She repre-

sents the ecstatic element in our relation to God, while
the disciples represent the reasonable element. Who
can blame the disciples for being angry about the im-
mense waste this woman has created? Certainly not a
deacon who has to take care of the poor, or a social
worker who knows the neediest cases and cannot help,
or a church administrator who collects money for important projects. Certainly the disciples would not be
blamed by a balanced personality who has his emotional life well under control and for whom it is worse
than nonsense, even criminal, to think of doing what
this woman did. Jesus felt differently and so did the
early Church. They knew that without the abundance
of the heart nothing great can happen. They knew that
religion within the limits of reasonableness is a mu-
tilated religion, and that calculating love is not love at
all. Jesus did not raise the question about how much
eros and how much *agape,* how much human passion
and how much understanding was motivating the
woman; He saw the abundant heart and He accepted
it without analyzing the different elements in it. There
are occasions when we must analyze ourselves and
others. And certainly we must know about the com-
plexity of all human motives. But this should not prevent us from accepting the waste of an uncalculated
self-surrender nor from wasting ourselves beyond the
limits of law and rationality.

The history of mankind is the history of men and
women who wasted themselves and were not afraid to
do so. They did not fear the waste of themselves, of
other men, of things in the service of a new creation.
They were justified, for they wasted all this out of the

fullness of their hearts. They wasted as God does in nature and history, in creation and salvation. The monsters of nature to which Jahweh points in His answer to Job—what are they but expressions of the divine abundance? Luther's God, who acts heroically and without rules—is He not the wasteful God who creates and destroys in order to create again? Has not Protestantism lost a great deal by losing the wasteful self-surrender of the saints and the mystics? Are we not in danger of a religious and moral utilitarianism which always asks for the reasonable purpose—the same question as that of the disciples in Bethany? There is no creativity, divine or human, without the holy waste which comes out of the creative abundance of the heart and does not ask, "What use is this?"

We know that lack of love in our early years is mentally destructive. But do we know that the lack of occasions to waste ourselves is equally dangerous? In many people there has been an abundance of the heart. But laws, conventions, and a rigid self-control have repressed it and it has died. People are sick not only because they have not received love but also because they are not allowed to give love, to waste themselves. Do not suppress in yourselves or others the abundant heart, the waste of self-surrender, the Spirit who trespasses all reason. Do not greedily preserve your time and your strength for what is useful and reasonable. Keep yourselves open for the creative moment which may appear in the midst of what seemed to be waste. Do not suppress in yourselves the impulse to do what the woman at Bethany did. You will be reproached by the disciples as the woman was. But Jesus was on her side and He is also on yours. Most of those who are great in the kingdom of God followed her, and the disciples, the reasonable Christians in all periods of history, will remember you as they have remembered her.

Jesus connects this anointing of His body with His death. There is an anointing of kings when they begin their reign and there is an anointing of corpses as a last gift of the living to the dead. Jesus speaks of the latter kind of anointing although He might easily have spoken of the former. In so doing, He turns both the ecstasy of the woman and the reasonableness of the disciples into something else. By His death the reasonable morality of the disciples is turned into a paradox: the Messiah, the Anointed One, must waste Himself in order to become the Christ. And the ecstatic self-surrender of the woman is tested by the ignominious perishing of the object of her unlimited devotion. In both cases we are asked to accept an act more radical, more divine, more saving than either ecstatic waste or reasonable service. The Cross does not disavow the sacred waste, the ecstatic surrender. It is the most complete and the most holy waste. And the Cross does not disavow the purposeful act, the reasonable service. It is the fulfillment of all wisdom within the plan of salvation. In the self-surrendering love of the Cross, reason and ecstasy, moral obedience and sacred waste are united. May we have the abundance of heart to waste ourselves as our reasonable service!

7

PRINCIPALITIES AND POWERS

For I am sure that neither death, nor life, nor angels, nor principalities, nor things present, nor things to come, nor powers, nor height, nor depth, nor anything else in all creation, will be able to separate us from the love of God in Christ Jesus our Lord.

ROMANS 8:38-39.

THESE WORDS ARE AMONG THE MOST powerful ever written. Their sound is able to grasp human souls in desperate situations. In my own experience they have proved to be stronger than the sound of exploding shells, of weeping at open graves, of the sighs of the sick, of the moaning of the dying. They are stronger than the self-accusation of those who are in despair about themselves and they prevail over the permanent whisper of anxiety in the depth of our being. What is it that makes these words so powerful?

It is not their literal meaning, for in many respects that is strange to us. The angels and principalities, the height and depth, and even life and death point to the constellations of the stars which, according to ancient beliefs, determine the fate of man and history. Men are in their power, driven by fear and fighting for courage, sometimes victorious, more often defeated. This was the predicament of the men to whom Paul was speaking. Several times in his letters he sums up the meaning of Christianity in the message that Christ has conquered these powers which govern the world, but nowhere does he affirm it as triumphantly as in the beautiful and powerful words to the Romans.

If these words have power over our souls in our time, they must say something which we feel to be true, even if we do not share the ancient belief in the stars and their constellations. They name the powers in whose bondage we all are and with us all men in all periods of history, and the whole of creation. And they show us that which can give us the certainty that these powers do not prevail against us, that they are conquered and that we can participate in the victory over them.

Who, in recent years, and indeed in our whole century, does not feel the irresistible forces which determine our historical and personal destiny? They drive nations and individuals into insoluble conflicts, internal and external; into arrogance and insanity, into revolt and despair, into inhumanity and self-destruction. Each of us is involved in these conflicts and driven to a greater or lesser degree by these forces. The personal life of each of us is in some way determined by them. No security is guaranteed to anyone; no house, no work, no friend, no family, no country anywhere in the world is safe, no plans are certain of fulfillment, all hopes are threatened. This is not a new state of things in human history. But what is new is that during a few years of comparative safety, we had forgotten that this is the true state of things. Now we see it again everywhere because suddenly we are living in its midst in every part of the earth.

Driven by the forces of fate, we ask the question mankind has always asked: What lies behind all this; what is its meaning; how can we endure it?

Long before the Christian era people spoke of the divine providence at work behind the driving forces of life and history. And in Christianity the words of Jesus about the birds of the air and the lilies of the field, and his command not to be anxious about tomorrow, have strengthened the faith in providence. It became the most common belief of Christian people. It gave them courage in danger, consolation in sorrow, hope among ruins. But more and more this faith lost its depth. It became a matter-of-course and was deprived of the overwhelming, surprising and triumphant character it has in the words of Paul.

When the German soldiers went into the First World War most of them shared the popular belief in a nice God who would make everything work out for the best. Actually, everything worked out for the worst, for the nation and for almost everyone in it. In the trenches of the war, the popular belief in personal providence was gradually broken and in the fifth year of war nothing was left of it. During and after the Second World War similar developments took place in this country. In the political tensions and fears of the last decade the belief in historical providence also broke down. The confidence, shared by large groups in this country, that in history everything will eventually turn out for the best, has almost disappeared. Today not much of it is left.

Neither the personal nor the historical belief in providence had depth or a real foundation. These beliefs were products of wishful thinking and not of faith. Faith in providence is not a *part* of the Christian faith —a part which is easier to grasp than the other parts. It is not the case, as an old country parson once told me, that people firmly believe in divine providence, but that the higher contents of the Christian faith, sin and salvation, Christ and the Church, are strange to them. If this is so, then the meaning of providence must also be strange to them and their belief in it is due to break down as such beliefs have in the storms of our century. *Faith in providence is faith altogether.* It is the courage to say yes to one's own life and life in general, in spite of the driving forces of fate, in spite of the insecurities of daily existence, in spite of the catastrophes of existence and the breakdown of meaning.

It is of such courage that Paul speaks in our text. But first he speaks of the powers which try to make this courage impossible. What do these powers do? They separate us from the love of God. This sentence is surprising. We would point to the dangers of pain and death which threaten our life day by day. Paul is certainly not unaware of them. He enumerates them as "tribulation or distress or persecution or famine or nakedness or peril or the sword." But he feels himself to be a conqueror of them all. And then he starts again and names the powers which threaten to separate us from the love of God. There is something mysterious about these powers. They do not have evil names like those which Paul has previously listed; most of them have glorious names—"angels," "principalities," "life" and "height." Why are they the ones which are most threatening? It is because they are always at work in every moment of our lives and because they have a double face. They are the powers which rule the world and they rule it for good and for evil. They grasp us by the good they bring and they destroy us by the evil they contain. This is the reason that they are more dangerous than the obvious evils. This is the reason that the triumph over them is the ultimate test which proves that Jesus is the Christ, the bringer of the new state of things.

Let us look into their nature, not as if they were strangers to us but as the driving powers of our own being. "Angels and principalities" are the names of some of them. Both of these words point to the same reality, a reality which has little in common with the nice winged babies who appear in most popular pictures of angels. They point to realities which are simultaneously both glorious and terrible; realities full of beauty and full of destructiveness. What are these realities? We do not have to look far to discover them. They are in all of us, in our own families, in our own nation, in our world. By what signs do we recognize them? By a mixture of irresistible fascination and unconquerable anxiety. The name of one of these powers with an angelic face is love. The poetry of all languages abounds in the praise of this principality ruling over the life of all men. Its angelic face appears in pictures and statues, its angelic beauty sounds through music, its divine fascination is expressed in the figures of pagan gods and goddesses. And at the same time, all works of art, and all myths are full of the tragic and deadly works of the angel of love. Fascination and fear, joy and guilt, creation and destruction are united in this great ruler of our lives. And both the joy and the anxiety of love tend to separate us from the love of God; the one by attracting us away from God to itself, the other by throwing us into the darkness of despair in which we cannot see God any longer.

Another principality, angelic and demonic at the same time, is power. It has the severe manly beauty which we see in some pictures of the great archangels. It is itself a great angel, good and evil, just as love is a mighty principality, and it is the builder and protector of cities and nations, a creative force in every human enterprise, in every human community, in every human achievement. It is responsible for the conquest of nature, the organization of states, the execution of justice. Its mighty ally is another angelic figure, good and evil, namely, knowledge. We are all in their bondage. World history is the realm in which the reign of the angel of power is most manifest in all its glory and in all its tragedy. There is no need to say more about it to the people of our time. Every morning brings us news about this ruler of our world. And we all are grasped both by the angelic fascination of its creativity and by the demonic terror of its destructiveness in our personal lives as well as in the lives of our nations. And when power is allied with knowledge—a knowledge undreamed of ever before in the history of mankind—fascination as well as terror are infinitely increased. Both separate us from the love of God, the one driving us to the adoration of power and knowledge, the other driving us to cynicism and despair.

Paul mentions two other pairs of realities which may separate us from the love of God—"height and depth," and "things present and things to come." Everyone understands their meaning without guidance. But it is hard to exhaust the richness of this meaning. Height and depth are the highest and lowest points in the movements of the stars; they are the points of their greatest and least influence, for good and for evil. Height and depth are the moments in which a life process reaches its strongest realization, in vitality and success and power, and in which it reaches its weakest realization, perhaps its end. Height and depth are the moments of victory and defeat, of fulfillment and emptiness, of elevation and depression, of fascination and of anxiety. And both moments, height as well as depth, try to separate us from the love of God, the one by its light, the other by its darkness, both making God invisible.

"Things present and things to come"—the first points to the impact which the present makes upon us. It points to the seductive power of the present, to our refusal to look back or ahead when we are held in the grip of the acute enjoyment or the acute pain of the present moment. And "things to come" means the expectation of the new, the joy of the unexpected, the courage of the risk. But it also means the incalculable, the contingent, and the anxiety about the strange and unknown.

Let us close this enumeration with the pair of most threatening powers, with which Paul begins—"death and life." These two belong to each other. In every life death is always present; it works in body and soul from the moment of conception to the moment of dissolution. It is present at the beginning of our lives just as much as at their end. At the moment of our birth we begin to die, and we continue to do so daily, throughout our lives. Growth is death, because it undermines the conditions of life even while it is increasing life. But not to grow is immediate death. All of us stand between the fascination of life and the anxiety of death, and sometimes between the anxiety of life and the fascination of death. Death and life are the greatest, the all-embracing powers, which try to separate us from the love of God.

We have looked at the powers which rule the world and over which the faith in providence must triumph. What is this faith? It is certainly not the belief that everything will turn out well in the end. It is not the belief that everything follows a preconceived plan, whether we call the planner God or Nature or Fate. Life is not a machine well-constructed by its builder and running on according to the forces and laws of its own machinery. Life, personal and historical, is a creative and destructive process in which freedom and destiny, chance and necessity, responsibility and tragedy are mixed with each other in everything and in every moment. These tensions, ambiguities and conflicts make life what it is. They create the fascination and the horror of life. They drive us to the question of a courage which can accept life without being conquered by it, and this is the question of providence.

But let us now drop the word "providence" with all its false connotations and look at what it really means. It means the courage to accept life in the power of that

which is more than life. Paul calls it the love of God.
This love, certainly, is above the angelic-demonic figure
of love of which we spoke. This love is the ultimate
power of union, the ultimate victory over separation.
Being united with it enables us to stand above life in
the midst of life. It enables us to accept the double-
faced rulers of life, their fascination and their anxiety,
their glory and their horror. It gives us the certainty
that no moment is possible in which we can be pre-
vented from reaching the fulfillment towards which all
life is striving. This is the courage to accept life in the
power of that in which life is rooted and overcome.

And if you now ask how this is possible, we turn
again to Paul's hymn and find there two answers. He
concludes his list of the ruling powers with the words,
". . . nor anything else in all *creation*." The powers
of this world are *creatures* as we are. They are no more
than we, they are limited. We are united with that
which is not creature and whose creative ground no
creature can destroy; then we know they cannot destroy
the *meaning* of our lives even if they can destroy our
lives. And this gives us the certainty that no creature
can destroy the meaning of life universal, in nature as
well as history, of which we are a part, even though
history and the whole universe should destroy themselves tomorrow. No creature can keep us from this
ultimate courage. None? Perhaps one—ourselves. Against
all the powers and principalities, including life and
death, the courage to maintain the unity with God
stands firm. But it falls when guilt separates us from
the love of God. Then we cannot face death, because
the sting of death is sin; we cannot face life because

guilt drives life into tragic self-destruction; we cannot face love because love is corrupted by greed; and we cannot face power because it is corrupted by cruelty. We shy away from the past because it is polluted by guilt, and we shy away from the future because it may bring the fruits of past guilt, and we cannot rest in the present because it accuses us and expels us. We cannot stand the height because we are afraid of falling, and we cannot stand the depth because we feel responsible for our fall. The rulers of the world cannot achieve what an uneasy conscience can achieve—the undermining of our courage to accept life. Therefore, Paul's final message is: Not even your guilty conscience can separate you from the love of God. For the love of God means that God accepts him who knows that he is unacceptable. This is the meaning of Paul's closing words, "in Christ Jesus our Lord." He is the victor over the rulers of the world because He is the victor over our hearts. His image gives us the certainty that even our hearts, our self-accusation, our despair about ourselves cannot separate us from the love of God, the ultimate unity, the source and ground of the courage to accept life.

PART II

The New Being as Freedom

8

"WHAT IS TRUTH?"

And the Word became flesh and dwelt among us, full of grace and truth; . . . For the law was given through Moses; grace and truth came through Jesus Christ.

JOHN 1:14, 17.

Why do you not understand what I say? . . . you are of your father the devil. . . . He was a murderer from the beginning, and has nothing to do with truth, because there is no truth in him. When he lies, he speaks according to his own nature, for he is a liar and the father of lies.

JOHN 8:43, 44.

Pilate said to him, "So you are a king?" Jesus answered, "You say that I am a king. For this I was born, and for this I have come into the world, to bear witness to the truth. Every one who is of the truth hears my voice." Pilate said to him, "What is truth?"

JOHN 18:37, 38.

Jesus said to him, "I am the way, and the truth, and the life."

JOHN 14:6.

He who does what is true, comes to the light.

JOHN 3:21.

*And I will pray the Father, and he will give you
. . . the Spirit of truth, whom the world cannot receive, because it neither sees him nor knows him;
you know him, for he dwells with you, and will be
in you.*

JOHN 14:16, 17.

*When the Spirit of truth comes, he will guide you
into all the truth.*

JOHN 16:13.

*Let us love one another; for love is of God, and he
who loves is born of God and knows God. He who
does not love does not know God; for God is love.*

I JOHN 4:7, 8.

*Jesus then said to the Jews who had believed in
Him, "If you continue in my word, you are truly my
disciples, and you will know the truth, and the truth
will make you free."*

JOHN 8:31, 32.

IN THE ABOVE PASSAGES THERE ARE
words in which Jesus speaks about truth. Another of
these words shall be the center of our meditation, the
word in which He combines truth and freedom: "The
truth will make you free."

The question of truth is universally human; but like

everything human it was first manifest on a special place in a special group. It was the Greek mind in which the passionate search for truth was most conspicuous; and it was the Greek world in which, and to which, the Gospel of John was written. The words, here said by Jesus, are, according to ancient custom, put into His mouth by the evangelist who wanted to show the answer of Christianity to the central question of the Hellenic mind: the question of truth. The answer is given also to us, for we, too, ask the question of truth. And some of us ask it as passionately, and sometimes as desperately, as the Greeks did.

It is often at an early age that we are moved by the desire for truth. When I, myself, as a fifteen-year-old boy received the words of our text as the motto for my future life from the confirming minister, who happened to be my father, I felt that this was just what I was looking for; and I remember that I was not alone in my group with this longing for truth. But I also observed, in myself and in others, that the early passion for truth is due to be lost in the adolescent and adult years of our lives. How does this happen?

The truth the child first receives is imposed upon him by adults, predominantly by his parents. This cannot be otherwise; and he cannot help accepting it. The passion for truth is silenced by answers which have the weight of undisputed authority, be it that of the mother or the father, or an older friend, or a gang, or the representatives of a social pattern. But sooner or later the child revolts against the truth given to him. He denies the authorities either all together, or one in the name of the other. He uses the teachers against the parents, the gang against the teachers, a friend against the gang, society against the friend.

This revolt is as unavoidable as was his early dependence on authority. The authorities gave him something to live on, the revolt makes him responsible for the truth he accepts or rejects.

But whether in obedience or in revolt, the time comes when a new way to truth is opened to us, especially to those in academic surroundings: The way of scholarly work. Eagerly we take it. It seems so safe, so successful, so independent of both authority and willfulness. It liberates from prejudices and superstitions; it makes us humble and honest. Where else, besides in scholarly work, should we look for truth? There are many in our period, young and old, primitive and sophisticated, practical and scientific, who accept this answer without hesitation. For them scholarly truth is truth altogether. Poetry may give beauty, but it certainly does not give truth. Ethics may help us to a good life, but it cannot help us to truth. Religion may produce deep emotions, but it should not claim to have truth. Only science gives us truth. It gives us new insights into the way nature works, into the texture of human history, into the hidden things of the human mind. It gives a feeling of joy, inferior to no other joy. He who has experienced this transition from darkness, or dimness, to the sharp light of knowledge will always praise scientific truth and understanding and say with some great medieval theologians, that the principles through which we know our world are the eternal divine light in our souls. And yet, when we ask those who have finished their studies in our colleges and universities whether they have found there a truth which is relevant to their lives they will answer with hesitation. Some will say that they have lost what they had of relevant truth; others will say that they don't care for such a truth because life goes on from day to day without it. Others will tell you of a person, a book, an event outside their studies which gave them the feeling of a truth that matters. But they all will agree that it is not the scholarly work which can give truth relevant for our life.

Where else, then, can we get it? "Nowhere," Pilate answers in his talk with Jesus. "What is truth?" he asks, expressing in these three words his own and his contemporaries' despair of truth, expressing also the despair of truth in millions of our contemporaries, in schools and studios, in business and professions. In all of us, open or hidden, admitted or repressed, the despair of truth is a permanent threat. We are children of our period as Pilate was. Both are periods of disintegration, of a world-wide loss of values and meanings. Nobody can separate himself completely from this reality, and nobody should even try. Let me do something unusual from a Christian standpoint, namely, to express praise of Pilate—not the unjust judge, but the cynic and sceptic; and of all those amongst us in whom Pilate's question is alive. For in the depth of every serious doubt and every despair of truth, the passion for truth is still at work. Don't give in too quickly to those who want to alleviate your anxiety about truth. Don't be seduced into a truth which is not really your truth, even if the seducer is your church, or your party, or your parental tradition. Go with Pilate, if you cannot go with Jesus; but go in seriousness with him!

Twofold are the temptations to evade the burden of asking for the truth that matters. The one is the way of those who claim to have the truth and the other is the way of those who do not care for the truth. The first ones are called "the Jews" in our gospel. They point to their tradition which goes back to Abraham. Abraham is their father; so they have all truth, and do not need to be worried by the question which they encounter in Jesus. Many among us, Christians and secularists, are "Jews" in the sense of the Fourth Gospel. They point to *their* tradition which goes back to the Church Fathers, or to the popes, or to the Reformers, or to the makers of the American Constitution. Their church or their nation is their mother, so they have all truth and do not need to worry about the question of truth. Would Jesus tell them, perhaps, what He told the Jews—that even if the church or the nation is their mother, they carry with them the heritage of the father of untruth; that the truth they have is not the truth which makes free? Certainly there is no freedom where there is self-complacency about the truth of one's own beliefs. There is no freedom where there is ignorant and fanatical rejection of foreign ideas and ways of life. There is not freedom but demonic bondage where one's own truth is called the ultimate truth. For this is an attempt to be like God, an attempt which is made in the name of God.

There is the second way of avoiding the question of truth—the way of not caring for it, of indifference. It is the way of the majority of the people today, as well

as at the time of Jesus. Life, they say to themselves, is
a mixture of truth, half-truth and falsehood. It is quite
possible to live with his mixture, to muddle through
most of the difficulties of life without asking the question of a truth that matters ultimately. There may be
boundary situations, a tragic event, a deep spiritual fall,
death. But as long as they are far removed, the question
of truth can also stay far away. Hence, the common
attitude—a little bit of Pilate's scepticism, especially in
things which it is not dangerous today to doubt, as, for
instance, God and the Christ; and a little bit of the
Jew's dogmatism, especially in things which one is re-
quested to accept today, as, for instance, an economic
or political way of life. In other words, some scepticism
and some dogmatism, and a shrewd method of balanc-
ing them liberate one from the burden of asking the
question of ultimate truth.

But those of us who dare to face the question of truth
may listen to what the Fourth Gospel says about it.
The first thing which strikes us is that the truth of which
Jesus speaks is not a doctrine but a reality, namely, He
Himself: "I *am* the truth." This is a profound transformation of the ordinary meaning of truth. For us,
statements are true or false; people may *have* truth or
not; but how can they *be* truth, even *the* truth? The
truth of which the Fourth Gospel speaks is a true reality—that reality which does not deceive us if we accept
it and live with it. If Jesus says, "I am the truth," he
indicates that in Him the true, the genuine, the ultimate reality is present; or, in other words, that God is
present, unveiled, undistorted, in His infinite depth, in
His unapproachable mystery. Jesus is not the truth be-

cause His teachings are true. But His teachings are
true because they express the truth which He Himself
is. He is more than His words. And He is more than
any word said about Him. The truth which makes us
free is neither the teaching of Jesus nor the teaching
about Jesus. Those who have called the teaching of
Jesus "the truth" have subjected the people to a servitude under the law. And most people like to live under
a law. They want to be told what to think and what
not to think. And they accept Jesus as the infallible
teacher and giver of a new law. But even the words of
Jesus, if taken as a law, are not the truth which makes
us free. And they should not be used as such by our
scholars and preachers and religious teachers. They
should not be used as a collection of infallible prescrip-
tions for life and thought. They *point* to the truth, but
they are not a law of truth. Nor are the doctrines about
Him the truth that liberates. I say this to you as somebody who all his life has worked for a true expression
of the truth which is the Christ. But the more one
works, the more one realizes that our expressions, including everything we have learned from our teachers
and from the teaching of the Church in all generations,
is not the truth that makes us free. The Church very
early forgot the word of our Gospel that He *is* the
truth; and claimed that her doctrines about Him are the
truth. But these doctrines, however necessary and good
they were, proved to be not the truth that liberates.
Soon they became tools of suppression, of servitude
under authorities; they became means to prevent the
honest search for truth—weapons to split the souls of
people between loyalty to the Church and sincerity to

truth. And in this way they gave deadly weapons to those who attacked the Church and its doctrines in the name of truth. Not everybody feels this conflict. There are masses of people who feel safe under doctrinal laws. They are safe, but it is the safety of him who has not yet found his spiritual freedom, who has not yet found his true self. It is the dignity and the danger of Protestantism that it exposes its adherents to the insecurity of asking the question of truth for themselves and that it throws them into the freedom and responsibility of personal decisions, of the right to choose between the ways of the sceptics, and those who are orthodox, of the indifferent masses, and Him who *is* the truth that liberates. For this is the greatness of Protestantism: that it points beyond the teachings of Jesus and beyond the doctrines of the Church to the being of Him whose being is the truth.

How do we reach this truth? "By doing it," is the answer of the Fourth Gospel. This does not mean being obedient to the commandments, accepting them and fulfilling them. Doing the truth means living out of the reality which is *He* who is the truth, making His being the being of ourselves and of our world. And again, we ask, "How can this happen?" "By remaining in Him" is the answer of the Fourth Gospel, *i.e.*, by participating in His being. "Abide in me and I in you," he says. The truth which liberates is the truth in which we participate, which is a part of us and we a part of it. True discipleship is participation. If the real, the ultimate, the divine reality which is His being becomes our being we are in the truth that matters.

And a third time we ask, "How can this happen?"

There is an answer to this question in our Gospel which may deeply shock us: "Every one who is of the truth hears my voice." Being "of the truth" means, coming from the true, the ultimate reality, being determined in one's being by the divine ground of all being, by that reality which is present in the Christ. If we have part in it, we recognize it wherever it appears; we recognize it as it appears in its fullness in the Christ. But, some may ask in despair: "If we have *no* part in it, if we are *not* of the truth, are we then forever excluded from it? Must we accept a life without truth, a life in error and meaninglessness? Who tells me that *I* am of the truth, that *I* have a chance to reach it?" Nobody can tell you; but there is one criterion: If you *seriously* ask the question, "Am I of the truth?" you *are* of the truth. If you do not ask it seriously, you do not really want, and you do not deserve, and you cannot get, an answer! He who asks seriously the question of the truth that liberates, is already on his way to liberation. He may still be in the bondage of dogmatic self-assurance but he has begun to be free from it. He may still be in the bondage of cynical despair, but he has already started to emerge from it. He may still be in the bondage of unconcern about the truth that matters, but his unconcern is already shaken. These all are of the truth and on their road to the truth.

On this road you will meet the liberating truth in many forms except in one form: you never will meet it in the form of propositions which you can learn or write down and take home. But you may encounter it in one sentence of a book or of a conversation or of a lecture, or even of a sermon. This sentence is not the

truth, but it may open you up for the truth and it may
liberate you from the bondage to opinions and prejudices and conventions. Suddenly, true reality appears
like the brightness of lightening in a formerly dark place.
Or, slowly, true reality appears like a landscape when
the fog becomes thinner and thinner and finally dis-
appears. New darknesses, new fogs will fall upon you;
but you have experienced, at least once, the truth and
the freedom given by the truth. Or you may be grasped
by the truth in an encounter with a piece of nature—
its beauty and its transitoriness; or in an encounter with
a human being in friendship and estrangement, in love,
in difference and hate; or in an encounter with yourself in a sudden insight into the hidden strivings of your
soul, in disgust and even hatred of yourself, in reconciliation with and acceptance of yourself. In these encounters you may meet the true reality—the truth which
liberates from illusions and false authorities, from en-
slaving anxieties, desires and hostilities, from a wrong
self-rejection and a wrong self-affirmation.

And it may even happen that you are grasped by the
picture and power of Him who is truth. There is no
law that this must happen. Many at all times and in
all places have encountered the true reality which is in
Him without knowing His name—as He Himself said.
They were of the truth and they recognized the truth,
although they had never seen Him who is the truth.
And those who have seen Him, the Christians in all
generations, have no guarantee that they participate in
the truth which He is. Maybe they were not of the
truth. Those, however, who are of the truth and who
have encountered Him who is the truth have one pre-

cious thing beyond the others: They have the point from which to judge all truth they encounter anywhere. They look at a life which never lost the communion with the divine ground of all life, and they look at a life which never lost the union of love with all beings.

And this leads to the last word which the man who has written the Gospel and the Letters of John has to say about truth: that the truth which liberates is the power of love, for God is love. The father of the lie binds us to himself by binding us to ourselves—or to that in us which is not our true self. Love liberates from the father of the lie because it liberates us from our false self to our true self—to that self which is grounded in true reality. Therefore, distrust every claim for truth where you do not see truth united with love; and be certain that you are of the truth and that the truth has taken hold of you only when love has taken hold of you and has started to make you free from yourselves.

9

FAITH AND UNCERTAINTY

IN HIS BOOK, *ON THE BONDAGE OF THE WILL*, Martin Luther writes, "What is more miserable than uncertainty!" He challenges the half-sceptical attitude of his great opponent, Erasmus of Rotterdam, who had declared that he would rather go over at once to the camp of the sceptics, if the authority of Scripture and the Church would permit him to do so. Luther demands *certainty* in the matter of our ultimate concern. He demands *assertions* and not sceptical possibilities or academic probabilities. "Take away assertions," he says, "and you take away Christianity." It is not the character of the Christian mind to avoid assertions, he declares. Every word of the prophets and the writers of the New Testament confirms his attitude and disproves that of Erasmus. Neither Jesus nor Paul nor John speaks in terms of probability or of accumulation of experiences. They make assertions with a certainty and an unshaken confidence about the truth of their message, which is often hard to stand and harder to understand for the modern mind. Paul writes to the Galatians, ". . . Even if we, or an angel from heaven, should preach to you a gospel contrary to that which we preached to you, let him be accursed." We feel a kind of resistance and even resentment against this unbroken certainty, the immediate consequence of which is the "Anathema" against heretics. Have we all become

Erasmians, consciously or unconsciously? Do we approach Christianity as just another possibility among so many others? As, perhaps, a probability, but by no means a certainty? Was it not embarrassing for all of us when Karl Barth, following the attitude of the Reformers, said his uncompromising "No!" to all attempts to approach God in terms of progressive assurance? Did we not hear in his words the voices of ancient and modern dictators? Is the fight between Paul and the Jewish perfectionists, between Augustine and the Pelagian rationalists, between Luther and the Erasmian humanists decided by a compromise in which, in reality, Paul, Augustine and Luther are defeated? I do not speak here of a theological defeat. I speak of a defeat in our hearts, in our lives, in the depths of our souls. Or can we still realize what Luther means when he exclaims, "What is more miserable than uncertainty!"

But let us look more exactly at the nature of that certainty which Paul and Luther defend. The words of Paul show clearly that it is not *self*—certainty: ". . . Even if *we* . . . should preach to you a gospel contrary to that which we preached to you. . . ." The truth of the gospel Paul has preached is not dependent on Paul. The certainty he has is not dependent on the changes in his personal experience. He can imagine that some day he might preach a distorted gospel; he can even imagine that an angel from heaven might bring another message than that which the Church has already received. He is not sure of himself and he is not even sure of angelic visions. But he is sure of the gospel, so sure that he places himself and the highest spiritual powers under the threat of a divine curse if he or they should distort the gospel. For, he continues, the gospel I preach is not a human affair; no man put it into my head. I, yet not I; my gospel and yet not my gospel; my certainty and yet not my certainty. This is a description of our situation before God which runs through the whole Bible and the confessions of all the great Christian witnesses. It *is* our certainty, but it is lost the moment we begin to regard it as our certainty. We are certain only as long as we look at the content of our certainty and not at the rational or irrational experiences in which we have received it. Looking at ourselves and our certainty as *ours,* we discover its weakness, its vulnerability to every critical thought; we discover the small amount of probability which our reasoning can give to the idea of God and to the reality of the Christ. We discover the contradictions in the emotional side of our religious life, its oscillation between ecstatic confidence and despairing doubt. But looking at God, we realize that all the shortcomings of our experience are of no importance. Looking at God, we see that we do not have Him as an object of our knowledge, but that He has us as the subject of our existence. Looking at God we feel that we cannot escape Him even by making Him an object of sceptical arguments or of irresistible emotions. We realize that in our uncertainty there is one fixed point of certainty, however we may name it and describe it and explain it. *We* may not comprehend, but we *are* comprehended. We may not grasp anything in the depth of our uncertainty, but that we are grasped by something ultimate, which keeps us in its grasp and from which we may strive in vain to escape, remains absolutely certain.

In this sense Luther speaks of Christian certainty. "By assertion," he writes, "I mean a constant adhering, affirming, defending and invincibly persevering." This certainty was not something he possessed as his own. Nobody has experienced the profundity of doubt more than he. The refuge in authority finally taken by both Augustine and Erasmus was made impossible by Luther. So were all possible arguments for religious truth and all confidence in his vocation as a reformer, in his religious strength and his accumulated experience. All these do not count in the ultimate uncertainty. But sometimes, when, in this worst of all Hells, the First Commandment, "I am the Lord, *thy* God," came to his mind, he knew that one certainty had not left him, and this was the only one which is ultimately needed.

Can we maintain this certainty in spite of the fundamental uncertainties which are the character of our period in religion as well as in all other realms of life? Can we maintain it in spite of our personal doubts and despairs and of our sceptical heritage? The answer to these questions does not depend on us. We can attain the certainty of the Reformers and Apostles whenever it is given to us to touch the Ground of our existence and to look beyond ourselves. When we have left behind all objective probabilities about God and the Christ, and all subjective approximations to God and the Christ, when all preliminary certainties have disappeared, the ultimate certainty may appear to us. And in the power of this certainty, though never secure and never without temptation, we may walk from certainty to certainty.

10

"BY WHAT AUTHORITY?"

One day, as he was teaching the people in the temple and preaching the gospel, the chief priests and the scribes with the elders came up and said to him, "Tell us by what authority you do these things, or who it is that gave you this authority." He answered them, "I also will ask you a question; now tell me, Was the baptism of John from heaven or from men?" And they discussed it with one another, saying, "If we say, 'From heaven,' he will say, 'Why did you not believe him?' But if we say, 'From men,' all the people will stone us; for they are convinced that John was a prophet." So they answered that they did not know whence it was. And Jesus said to them, "Neither will I tell you by what authority I do these things."

LUKE 20:1-8.

THE STORY WE HAVE READ WAS VERY important to the early Christians who preserved it for us. If we look at it superficially, no reason seems to exist for such a high valuation: the Jewish leaders tried to trap Jesus by a shrewd question, and Jesus trapped them by an even shrewder question. It is a pleasant anecdote. But is it more than this? Indeed, it is infinitely more. It does something surprising: it answers the fundamental question of prophetic religion by not answering it. An answer to the question of authority is refused by Jesus, but the way in which He refuses the answer *is* the answer.

Let us imagine that He had answered the question of the religious leaders about *His* authority by asking them about the sources of *their* authority! They could have replied easily and convincingly. The chief priests could have said, "The source of our authority is our consecration according to a tradition which goes back without interruption to Moses and Aaron. The sacred tradition of which we are a link from the past to the future gives us our authority."

And the scribes could have answered, "The source of our authority is our knowledge—beyond that of anybody else—of the Scriptures. We have studied them day and night since our early childhood, as a student of the Word of God must do. Because we are experts in interpreting the Holy Scriptures, we have authority."

And the elders could have said to Jesus, "The source of our authority is our acquisition of wisdom through many years, and our experience in applying it to the questions of the day. Our wisdom and our experience give us our authority."

And they all together would have said to Jesus, "But who are you, who are not consecrated and not studied in the Scriptures, and without the wisdom of age and the experience of practice? Which is the source of your authority? You have not only taught and preached, you have also acted as a radical, without our approval. You have driven out of the temple all who sold and bought, you have overturned the tables of the money-changers and the seats of those who sold pigeons. And you know yourself that they are necessary for the preservation of the temple and its cult, and for the performance of the sacrifices! By what authority have you turned against the religion as it has been given to us by Moses and by all generations since his time?"

Thus they could have answered His question. But Jesus does not ask them this question. He asks, "Was the baptism of John from heaven or from men?" And to this they could not answer. If they had said that it was from men, they would have hurt the popular feeling and perhaps even a feeling within themselves, that John was a prophet. But if they had said that he was from God, they would have established an authority beyond the threefold authority which they could claim for themselves. And this they did not want. *They*, who were called authorities, demanded that all authority be vested in *them*. Therefore, they did not accept John as a prophet, nor Jesus as the Christ. . . . Don't minimize the seriousness of this conflict. It was not simply a conflict between good and evil, between faith and unbelief. The conflict was much more profound and much more tragic than this!

Let us imagine that we ourselves were in the place of those who asked Jesus about the source of His authority. Let us imagine ourselves as the guardians of a great religious tradition, or as the unquestionable experts in a sphere of decisive importance for human existence, or as people who have learned through a

long experience to deal with matters of highest value.
And let us also assume that we had no function as
legally established authorities, and that somebody came
and spoke about the same things in quite a different
language and acted in the field of our authority in quite
a radical way; how would *we* react? And if the people
who saw and heard this man said of him what they
said about Jesus, that he teaches as one who has authority and not as we the established authorities, how
would *we* react? Would we not think: He confuses the
masses, he spreads dangerous doctrines, he undermines
well-proved laws and institutions, he introduces strange
modes of life and thought, he disrupts sacred ties, he
destroys traditions from which generations of men have
received discipline and strength and hope? It is our
duty to resist him and if possible to remove him! For
the sake of our people we must defend our consecrated
and tested authority against this man who cannot show
the source of the authority he claims." Could we be
blamed for such a reaction? And if not, can we blame
the authorities in Jerusalem for their reaction to Jesus?

We think of the Reformation. This was a moment in
the history of the Church in which the question of authority was once more in the center of events. Luther,
and consequently the whole Protestant world, broke
away from the Roman Church and from 1500 years of
Christian tradition when no agreement about the authority of the pope and the councils could be reached.
Here, again, someone had arisen who spoke and acted
with an authority the sources of which could not be
determined by legal means. And here also we must
ask, "Are the Catholic authorities who rejected him in

the name of their established authority to be blamed for it?" But if we do not *blame* them, we can ask them, "Why do *you* blame the Jewish authorities who did exactly the same as you did when the people said of the Reformers that they spoke with authority and not like the priests and monks?" Is the same thing so different if it is done by the Jewish high priest and if it is done by the Roman high priest? And one may ask the present-day Protestant authorities in Europe and in this country, "Are you certain that the insistence on your authority, on your tradition, and on your experience does not suppress the kind of authority which Jesus had in mind?"

And now we ask, "What does authority mean? What does it mean for man as man? What does it mean for our period and for each of us?"

First of all, it means that we are finite and in need of what the word "authority" really says: to be started and increased. It means that we are born, that we were infants and children, that we were completely dependent on those who gave us life and home and guidance and contents for soul and mind. We were not able to decide for ourselves for many years, and that made us dependent on authority and made authority a benefit for us. We accepted this authority without resistance, even if we rebelled on special occasions. And this authority became the basis for all other authorities. It gave strength to the authority of the older brother or sister, of the more mature friend or teacher, of the official, of the ruler, of the minister. And through them we have been introduced into the institutions and traditions in society, state and Church. Authority permeates, guides, shapes our lives. The acceptance of authority is the acceptance of what is given by those who have more than we. And our subjection to them and to what they stand for enables us to live in history, as our subjection to the laws of nature enables us to live in nature. And from the authority of the law is derived the authority of those who represent and administer it and who, for this reason, are called "the authorities."

Our daily life would be impossible without traditions of behavior and customs and the authority of those who have received them and surrendered them to us. Man's control of nature would be impossible without the tradition of knowledge and skill into which every new generation is introduced and which gives authority to those who are able to introduce us. Man's intellectual life—the language he uses, the songs he sings, the music he plays, the houses he builds, the pictures he paints, the symbols he creates—he has received through the authority of those who have participated in it before him. Man's religious life—the faith he holds, the cult he loves, the stories and legends he has heard, the commandments he tries to obey, the texts he knows by heart—all this is not created by him; he takes it from those who represent to him religious authority.

And if he revolts against the authorities which have shaped him, he does it with the tools he has received from them. The language of the revolutionary is formed by those against whom he revolts. The protest of the reformer uses the tradition against which he protests. Therefore, no absolute revolution is possible. If it is attempted, it fails immediately; and if a revolution succeeds, its leaders soon have to use forms and ideas created by the authorities of the past. This is true of the rebellion of the adolescent against the family authority as well as of the rebellion of new social groups against the authority of the established powers.

When we speak of human finitude, we usually think of man's transitoriness in time, of birth and death, of the vicissitudes which threaten him in every moment. But we are not only finite in that we are temporal, we are also finite in that we are historical and that means subject to authority, even if we rebel against it. We are thrown into existence, not only bodily, but also mentally. In no respect are we by ourselves, in no moment can we be by ourselves. He who tries to be without authority tries to be like God, who alone is by Himself. And like everyone who tries to be like God, he is thrown down to self-destruction, be it a single human being, be it a nation, be it a period of history like our own.

In our story, Jesus as well as His foes acknowledge authority. They struggle about *valid* authority, not about authority as such. And this is what we find everywhere in the Bible and the life of the Church. Paul fights with the original disciples, including Peter, about the foundations of apostolic authority. The bishops fight with the enthusiasts about the leadership in the Church. The popes fight with the princes about the ultimate source of political authority. The reformers fight with the hierarchs about the interpretation of the Bible. The theologians fight with the scientists about the criteria of ultimate truth. None of the struggling groups denies authority, but each of them denies the authority of the other group.

But if the authority is split in itself, which authority decides? Is not split authority the end of authority? Was not the split produced by the Reformation the end of the authority of the Church? Is not the split about the interpretation of the Bible the end of the Biblical authority? Is not the split between theologians and scientists the end of intellectual authority? Is not the split between father and mother the end of parental authority? Was not the split between the gods of polytheism the end of their divine authority? Is not the split in one's conscience the end of the authority of one's conscience? If one has to choose between different authorities, not *they* but *oneself* is ultimate authority for oneself, and this means: there is no authority for him.

This, however, creates the dreadful alternative of *our* historical period. If there is no authority, we must decide ourselves, each for himself. As finite beings we must act as if we were infinite, and since this is impossible, we are driven into complete insecurity, anxiety and despair. Or, unable to stand the loneliness of deciding for ourselves, we suppress the fact that there is a split authority. We subject ourselves to a definite authority and close our eyes against all other claims. The desire of most people to do this is very well known to those in power. They use the unwillingness of human beings to decide for themselves in order to preserve their power and to increase it. This is true of religious as well as of political powers. On this ground of human weakness the systems of authority are built in past and present.

"By what authority" do you do this? Jesus is asked.

And He answers not by answering but by pointing to the acting and speaking of John. Here, He tells the leaders of His nation, you see the rise of an authority without ritual or legal foundation. But you deny the possibility of it. So you deny both the Baptist and myself. You deny the possibility of an authority guaranteed by its inner power. You have forgotten that the only test of the prophets was the power of what they had to say. Listen to what the *people* say about us, namely, that *we* speak with authority and not as *you*, who are called the "authorities." That is what He tells them.

What would He say to us? He would not have to fight about His authority with the chief priests and the scribes and the elders of our day. In our time they all acknowledge Him. He would have to ask a quite different question of them. He would have to ask: "What is the nature of *my* authority for you? Is it like that of John the Baptist, or is it like that of the authorities who tried to remove me? Have you made the words of those who have witnessed to me, the Bible, the Church Fathers, the popes, the reformers, the creeds, into ultimate authorities? Have you done this in my name? And if so, do you not abuse my name? For whenever my name is remembered, my fight with those who were in authority is also remembered."

There is something in the Christian message which is opposed to established authority. There is something in the Christian experience which revolts against subjection to even the greatest and holiest experiences of the past. And this something is indicated in the question of Jesus, "Was the baptism of John from God or man?" and in His refusal to give an answer! That which

makes an answer impossible is the nature of an authority which is derived from God and not man. The place
where God gives authority to a man cannot be circum-
scribed. It cannot be legally defined. It cannot be put
into the fences of doctrines and rituals. It is here, and
you do not know where it comes from. You cannot derive it. You must be grasped by it. You must participate
in its power. This is the reason why the question of
authority never can get an ultimate answer. Certainly
there are many preliminary answers. There is no day
in our lives in which we do not give, silently or openly,
answers to the question of authority, saying mostly
"yes" and sometimes "no."

But an ultimate answer we cannot give. We only can
point to a reality, as Jesus does. And this is what our
religious leaders could and should do—the churches, and
the ministers, and the theologians, and every Christian
who acts as a priest to other Christians. They all can
raise their finger as Jesus did to John, and as John did
to Jesus. We all can point passionately, but not as established authorities, to the Crucified—as does the Baptist,
in the tremendous picture by the old painter Matthias
Grünewald. There his whole being is in the finger with
which he points to the Cross. This is the greatest symbol
of which I know for the true authority of the Church
and the Bible. They should not point to themselves but
to the reality which breaks again and again through
the established forms of their authority and through
the hardened forms of our personal experiences.

And once more we ask: "What does it mean that the
question of authority cannot get an ultimate answer?"
It would sound like a blasphemy if I said, "Because

God Himself cannot give an answer." It would sound
not blasphemous but conventional if I said, "Because
God is Spirit." Yet both sentences mean the same. God
who is Spirit cannot give an ultimate answer to the
question of authority. The churches, their leaders and
members, often ignore the infinite significance of the
words "God is Spirit." But the sharp eyes of the enemy
see what these words mean. Nietzsche calls the man who
first said that God is Spirit the first one of those who
have killed God. His profound insight into the human
soul made it certain to him that a God who is not cir-
cumscribed on a definite place, who does not answer
definitively the question of authority, cannot be accepted by most human beings. If he were right, we
either had to agree with him that there is no God left,
or we had to return to a God who tells us a definite
answer to the question of authority, and subjects us by
Divine order to an established religious authority as
the earthly representative of His own heavenly authority. But this God is not the God who is Spirit. Actually,
such a God is the heavenly image of the earthly authorities which use Him for the consecration of their own
power. This God is not the God of whom Jesus speaks
in our story.

The God who cannot answer the question of ultimate
authority because He is Spirit does not remove the
preliminary authorities with whom we live our daily
lives. He does not condemn us to the emptiness of an
adolescent who feels that the world must start with
himself. He does not deprive us of the protection of
those who have more wisdom and power than we have.
He does not isolate us from the community to which

we belong and which is a part of ourselves. But he denies ultimate significance to all these preliminary authorities, to all those who claim to be images of His authority and who distort God's authority into the oppressive power of a heavenly tyrant.

The God who does not answer the question of ultimate authority transforms the preliminary authorities into media and tools of Himself—of the God who is Spirit. Parental authority on earth is not the consecrated image of a parental authority in heaven, but it is the earliest tool through which the Spiritual qualities of order and self-control and love are mediated to us. Therefore, the parents must be and remain subjects of honor, but not of unconditional authority. Even God whom we call the Father in heaven cannot answer the ultimate question of authority. How could the parents?

The authority of wisdom and knowledge on earth is not the consecrated image of the authority of heavenly omniscience, but it is the tool through which the Spiritual qualities of humility and knowledge and wisdom are mediated to us. Therefore, the wise ones should be honored but not accepted as unconditional authorities.

The authorities in community and society, in nation and state, are not consecrated images of heavenly power and justice, but they are tools through which the Spiritual qualities of mutuality, understanding, righteousness, and courage can be mediated to us. Therefore, the social authorities should be accepted as guarantees of external order but not as those which determine the meaning of our lives.

The authority of the Church is not the consecrated earthly image of the Heavenly Ruler of the Church, but it is a medium through which the Spiritual substance of our lives is preserved and protected and reborn.

Even the authority of Jesus the Christ is not the consecrated image of the man who rules as a dictator, but it is the authority of him who emptied himself of all authority; it is the authority of the man on the Cross. It is one and the same thing, if you say that God is Spirit and that He is manifest on the Cross.

And you who are fighting *against* authorities and you who are searching *for* authorities, listen to the story in which Jesus fights against them and establishes an authority which cannot be established! Here is an answer, namely, that no answer can be given except the one that, beyond all preliminary authorities, you must keep yourselves open to the power of Him who is the ground and the negation of everything which is authority on earth and in Heaven! . . .

11

HAS THE MESSIAH COME?

Now there was a man in Jerusalem, whose name was Simeon, and this man was righteous and devout, looking for the consolation of Israel, and the Holy Spirit was upon him. And it had been revealed to him by the Holy Spirit that he should not see death before he had seen the Lord's Christ. And inspired by the Spirit he came into the temple; and when the parents brought in the child Jesus, to do for him according to the custom of the law, he took him up in his arms and blessed God and said,

"Lord, now lettest thou thy servant depart in
*   peace, according to thy word;*
for mine eyes have seen thy salvation
which thou has prepared in the presence of
*   all peoples,*
a light for revelation to the Gentiles,
and for glory to thy people Israel."

LUKE 2:25-32.

Then turning to the disciples [Jesus] said privately, "Blessed are the eyes which see what you see! For I tell you that many prophets and kings desired to see what you see, and did not see it, and to hear what you hear, and did not hear it."

LUKE 10:23-24.

A FEW DAYS AGO I HAD A TALK WITH a Jewish friend about the idea of the Messiah in Judaism and Christianity. We finally stated the difference in a way similar to the alternative put before Jesus by the disciples of John Baptist: "Are you the Coming One? Or are we to look out for someone else?" We agreed that the Jews are looking for someone else while the Christians assert that the "Coming One" has already come. The Christians say with Simeon: "Our eyes *have* seen His salvation." The Jews reply: "We have *not* seen His salvation, we are waiting for it." The Christians feel blessed, according to the words of Jesus, because they have seen the presence of the saving power within the world and history. The Jews consider such a feeling almost blasphemous, since, according to their faith, nothing of what they expect to happen in the Messianic age has actually happened. And when we defend our Christian faith they point to the fact that the world has not become better since the days of Hosea and Jeremiah, that the Jews—and with them the largest part of mankind—are suffering not less than they did two thousand years ago; that the prophetic visions of doom are more realistic today than they were in those days. It is hard to answer this; but we *must* answer it for not only the Jews, but also innumerable Christians and non-Christians, our friends and our children, and something in ourselves ask these questions.

It is hard to answer them. What, for instance, *can* we answer when our children ask us about the child in the Manger while in some parts of the world all children "from two years old and under" have died and are dying, not by an order of Herod, but by the ever-increasing cruelty of war and its results in the Christian era and by the decrease of the power of imagination in the Christian people. Or, what can we answer the Jews when the remnants of the Jewish people, returning from death-camps, worse than anything in Babylon, cannot find a resting place anywhere on the surface of the earth, and certainly not amongst the great Christian nations? Or, what can we answer Christians and non-Christians who have realized that the fruit of centuries of Christian technical and social civilization is the imminent threat of a complete and universal self-destruction of humanity? And what answer can we give to ourselves when we look at the unhealed and unsaved stage of our own lives after the message of healing and salvation has been heard at every Christmas for almost two thousand years?

Should we say that *the world,* of course, is unsaved but that there are men and women in all generations who are saved *from* the world? But this is not the message of Christmas. All those in the Christmas legend who expect the Christ and receive the divine are looking out for the salvation of Israel and of the Gentiles and of the world. For all of them, and for Jesus Himself, and for the apostles, the kingdom of God, the universal salvation is at hand. But if this was the expectation, has it not been utterly refuted by reality?

This question is as old as the Christian message itself

and the answer is equally old, as our texts indicate.
Jesus takes His disciples aside and speaks privately to
them when He praises them because they see what they
are seeing. The presence of the Messiah is a mystery;
it cannot be said to everybody, and it cannot be seen
by everybody, but only by those like Simeon who are
driven by the Spirit. There is something surprising, unexpected about the appearance of salvation, something
which contradicts pious opinions and intellectual demands. *The mystery of salvation is the mystery of a
child.* So it was anticipated by Isaiah, by the ecstatic
vision of the sibyl and by the poetic vision of Virgil,
by the doctrines of mysteries and by the rites of those
who celebrated the birth of the new eon. They all felt
as did the early Christians, that the event of salvation
is the birth of a child. A child is real and not yet real,
it is *in* history and not yet historical. Its nature is visible
and invisible, it is here and not yet here. And just this
is the character of salvation. *Salvation has the nature
of a child.* As Christendom remembers every year, in
the most impressive of its festivals, the child Jesus, so
salvation, however visible it may be, remains always
also invisible. He who wants a salvation which is *only*
visible cannot see the divine child in the Manger as he
cannot see the divinity of the Man on the Cross and
the paradoxical way of all divine acting. Salvation is
a child and when it grows up it is crucified. Only he
who can see power under weakness, the whole under
the fragment, victory under defeat, glory under suffering, innocence under guilt, sanctity under sin, life under
death can say: Mine eyes have seen thy salvation.

It is hard to say this in our days. But it always has

been hard and it always will be hard. It was and is and will be a mystery, the mystery of a child. And however deep the world might fall, even into utter self-destruction, as long as there are men they will experience this mystery and say: "Blessed are the eyes which see the things that we see."

12

"HE WHO BELIEVES IN ME . . ."

And Jesus cried out and said, "He who believes in me, believes not in me but in him who sent me. And he who sees me sees him who sent me. I have come as light into the world, that whoever believes in me may not remain in darkness. If any one hears my sayings and does not keep them, I do not judge him; for I did not come to judge the world but to save the world. He who rejects me and does not receive my sayings has a judge; the word that I have spoken will be his judge on the last day. For I have not spoken on my own authority; the Father who sent me has himself given me commandment what to say and what to speak. And I know that his commandment is eternal life. What I say, therefore, I say as the Father has bidden me."

JOHN 12:44-50.

"HE WHO BELIEVES IN ME, BELIEVES NOT in *me* but in him who sent me. . . ." These words follow a bitter complaint of the evangelist about the unbelief and half-belief of the people and their leaders. The words are introduced by the phrase: "Jesus cried out. . . ." He is making an almost desperate effort to be understood. And what He cries out is that believing in Him means not believing in *Him*. The argument of the unbelievers was—and is in all periods—that it is impossible to believe in Jesus of Nazareth as Jesus of Nazareth. Jesus declares: "This argument is valid. If people are asked to believe in me, they should not do so. But they are not asked any such thing! They are asked to believe in Him who has sent me, who is greater than I and with whom I am one. I have not spoken on my own authority," He continues. "If I did so, the unbelievers would be right."

There are many authorities in past and present. Why accept one and not another? Why accept any authority? As Jesus the man Jesus is neither an authority nor an object of faith. None of His superior qualities—neither His religious life, nor His moral perfection, nor His profound insights—make Him an object of faith or the ultimate authority. On this basis, He says, He does not judge anyone. If He did, he would be a tyrant who imposes Himself and His greatness on others, thus destroying instead of saving them.

What about our preaching? When we use the name of Jesus, do we not often try to force upon those to whom we are speaking and upon ourselves something great besides God? Do we always make it clear that believing in Him does not mean believing in *Him?* If not, are we not working for destruction more than for salvation?

It seems that the Christian painters knew more about this than we often do. They did not present a picture of Jesus of Nazareth as Jesus of Nazareth. They painted

Him as the infant of Bethlehem who contains the whole universe, though "lying now in Mary's lap," as Luther sings. Through His infantile traits shines the power of the Lord of the world. Or they painted Him as the visible bearer of the divine majesty in those great mosaics where every piece of His gown is transparent for the infinite depth He represents and expresses. Or they painted Him as the Crucified who does not suffer as an individual man, but as He who stands for both the suffering universe and the divine love which participates in its suffering. Or they painted Him as the bringer of the new æon who controls the powers of nature, the souls of men, the demonic forces of disease, insanity, and death. But they did not give Him individual traits, did not make him a representative of a psychological type or of a sociological group.

Look at the pictures of the Sistine Chapel. Michaelangelo gave a special character to every prophet, to every sibyl. But when he painted Jesus as the ultimate judge, only an irresistible divine-human power appears.

When in our time Jesus became an object of biographical and psychological essays and was portrayed as a fanatic and neurotic, or as a pious sufferer, or as a social benefactor, or as a moral example, or as a religious teacher, or as a mass leader—He ceased to be the one in whom we can believe, for He ceased to be the one in whom we do *not* believe, if we believe in Him. He was no longer the Jesus who is the Christ.

We cannot pray to anyone except to God. If Jesus is someone besides God, we cannot and should not pray to Him. Many Christians, many among us, cannot find a way of joining honestly with those who pray to Jesus

Christ. Something in us is reluctant, something which is genuine and valid, the fear of becoming idolatrous, the fear of being split in our ultimate loyalty, the fear of looking at two faces instead of at the one divine face.

But he who sees *Him* sees the Father. There are not two faces. In the face of Jesus the Christ, God "makes His face to shine upon us." For nothing is left in the face of Jesus the Christ which is only Jesus of Nazareth, which is only the face of *one* individual besides others. Everything in His countenance is transparent to Him who has sent Him. Therefore, and therefore alone, can we sing at Christmas-time: "O come, let us adore Him!"

13

YES AND NO

Jesus Christ . . . was not Yes and No; but in him it is always Yes. For all the promises of God find their Yes in him.

II CORINTHIANS 1:19, 20.

A CHANGE IN HIS TRAVELING PLANS and the angry reaction of the Corinthian Christians to this change is used by Paul for profound and far-reaching assertions about Jesus "the Christ": "In him it is always Yes, he is not Yes and No." This reminds us by contrast of the words of a great Protestant mystic who has said that in Yes and No all things consist, and of philosophers and theologians who are convinced that truth can only be expressed through No and Yes, and above all of Paul's own central doctrine that God justifies the sinner, that He says "yes" to him to whom He says a radical "no" at the same time. And does not Paul in this second letter to the Corinthians formulate the Yes and No in a most paradoxical way: "Unknown and yet well known, dying and behold we live, having nothing and yet possessing everything." This certainly is Yes and No. But in the Christ, he says, there is not Yes and No. Really not? Do we not come from Good Friday

101

to Easter, which point to the deepest No and the highest Yes—that of the death and life of the Christ?

Yes and No: This certainly is the law of all life, but not Yes alone and not No alone. Yes alone is the advice of a self-deceiving confidence which soon will be shaken by the No of the three gray figures: emptiness, guilt, death. No alone is the advice of a self-deceiving despair whose hidden Yes to itself is manifest in its self-seclusion and its resistance against the Yes of love and communion. And further, Yes and No is the law of all truth. Not Yes alone and not No alone! Yes alone is the arrogance which claims that its limited truth is the ultimate truth, but which reveals by its fanatical self-affirmation how many hidden No's are present in its ground. No alone is the resignation which denies any ultimate truth but which shows by its self-complacent irony against the biting power of every word of truth how strong the Yes to itself is that underlies its ever-repeated No.

Truth as well as life unite Yes and No, and only the courage which accepts the infinite tension between Yes and No can have abundant life and ultimate truth. How is such a courage possible? It is possible because there is a Yes above the Yes and No of life and of truth. But it is a Yes which is not ours. If it were ours, even our greatest, our most universal and most courageous Yes, it would be contrasted by another No. This is the reason why no theology and no philosophy, not even a theology or philosophy of "Yes and No" is ultimate truth. In the moment in which it is expressed, it is contradicted by another philosophy and another theology. Not even the message of Yes and No, be it said by Kierkegaard or by Luther or by Paul, can escape its

No. There is only one reality where there is not Yes and No but only Yes: Jesus as the Christ. First He also stands under the No, as completely as a being can stand; this is the meaning of the Cross. Everything of Him which is only the expression of a finite life or a finite truth stands with all life and all truth under the No. Therefore, we are not asked to accept Him as the unquestionable teacher or as the always fitting example, but we are told that in Him all promises of God have become real, and that in Him a life and a truth which is beyond Yes and No has become manifest. This is the meaning of "Resurrection." The No of death is conquered and the Yes of life is transcended by that which has appeared in Him. A life which is not balanced by death, a truth which is not balanced by error is visible in His being. He shows the final Yes without another No. This is the Easter message; this is the Christian message altogether. And this is the ground of a courage which can stand the infinite tension between Yes and No in everything finite, even in everything religious and in everything Christian.

Paul points to the fact that the Christians say Amen through Christ. One cannot say Amen to anything except the reality which is the Christ. Amen is the formula of confirmation, the expression of ultimate certitude. There is no ultimate certitude except the life which has conquered its death and the truth which has conquered its error, the Yes which is beyond Yes and No.

Paul points to that which gives us such a certainty: It is not an historical report, but it is the participation *in* Christ, in whom we are established, as he says, who has given us the guarantee of His Spirit in our hearts.

We can stand the Yes and No of life and truth because we participate in the Yes beyond Yes and No, because we are *in* it, as it is *in* us. We are participants of His resurrection; therefore, we can say the ultimate Yes, the Amen beyond *our* Yes and *our* No.

14

"WHO ARE MY MOTHER AND
MY BROTHERS . . .?"

*Then he went home; and the crowd came together
again, so that they could not even eat. And when his
friends heard it, they went out to seize him; for they
said, "He is beside himself."*

MARK 3:19-21.

*And his mother and his brothers came; and stand-
ing outside they sent to him and called him. And a
crowd was sitting about him; and they said to him,
"Your mother and your brothers are outside, asking
for you." And he answered, "Who are my mother
and my brothers?" And looking around on those who
sat about him, he said, "Here are my mother and my
brothers! Whoever does the will of God is my
brother, and sister, and mother."*

MARK 3:31-35.

FOR MOST OF THOSE WHO GO AWAY TO
a university to study, it is not the first time that they
leave the home of their parents. But for all of them it
is an important step on their own independent way of

life. Every step on this road brings them farther away from the place from which they came, the family into which they were born. The first moves towards independence occur very early in life—as exemplified in the story of the twelve-year-old Jesus in the temple. And none of these moves is without pain and tragic guilt —as indicated in the anxiety of the parents of Jesus and the reproaches they made to Him. But only after Jesus has begun His public activities the depth of the gap between Him and His family becomes fully manifest. In the story which we have just read and which is recorded by the three first Gospels, Jesus uses the family relations as symbols for a relation of a higher order, for the community of those who do the will of God. Something unconditional breaks into the conditional relations of the natural family and creates a community which is as intimate and as strong as the family relations, and at the same time infinitely superior to it. The depth of this gap is emphasized in the attempt of His family to seize Him and to bring Him home because of His extraordinary behavior which makes them believe that He is out of His mind. And the gap is strongly expressed in His saying that He who loves father and mother more than Him cannot be His disciple, words even sharpened in Luke's version, where everyone is rejected by Him who does not "hate" father and mother and wife and children and brothers and sisters—and his own life.

All these words cut with divine power through the natural relation between the members of the family whenever these relations claim to be ultimates. They cut through the bondage of age-old traditions and conventions and their unconditional claims; they cut through the consecration of the family ties by sacramental or other laws which make them equal to the ties between those who belong to the new reality in the Christ. The family is no ultimate! The family relations are not unconditional relations. The consecration of the family is not a consecration for the final aim of man's existence. We can imagine the revolutionary character of such sayings in face of the religions and cultures of mankind. We can hardly measure their disturbing character in face of what has happened century after century within the so-called Christian nations—with the support of the Christian churches who could not stand the radical nature of the Christian message in this as in other respects. However, in spite of its radicalism, the Christian message does not request the dissolution of the family. It affirms the family and limits its significance. Jesus takes up the prophecy of Micah, that in the last days "brother will deliver up brother to death, and the father his child, and children will rise against parents and have them put to death." It belongs to periods in which the demonic powers get hold of the world, that the family community is turned into its opposite. But when Jesus uses this prophecy, He adds, "And you will be hated by all for my name's sake." The same words which point to the demonic disruption of the family are used to describe its inescapable divine disruption. This is the profound ambiguity of the Biblical teaching about the family.

Now let us look into our own situation. We cannot cut the ties with our family without being guilty. But the question is: Is it willfulness which demonically disrupts the family communion, or is it the step toward independence and one's own understanding of the will of God which divinely liberates us from the bondage to our family? We never know the answer with certainty. We must risk tragic guilt in becoming free from father and mother and brothers and sisters. And we know today better than many generations before us what that means, how infinitely difficult it is and that nobody does it without carrying scars in his soul his whole life. For it is not only the real father or mother or brother or sister from whom we must become free in order to come into our own. It is something much more refined, the image of them, which from our earliest childhood has impregnated our souls. The real father, the real mother may let us go free, although this is by no means the rule in Christian families. But even if they have the wisdom to do it, their images can prevent us from doing what the will of God is in a concrete situation, namely, to do acts in which love, power and justice are united. Their image may prevent us from love by subjection to law. It may prevent us from having power by weakening our personal center. It may prevent us from exercising justice by blinding us to a concrete situation and its demands. And the same happens with the images of brothers and sisters. Although it is easier to become free from them in an external sense, they may hiddenly produce decisions which determine for the worse whole periods of our lives.

But do not mistake me! Opposition and revolt are not yet freedom. They are unavoidable stages on the way to freedom. But they create another servitude if they are not overcome as much as the early dependence must be overcome. How can this happen? Certainly, in pathological cases, psychotherapy is needed, as Jesus Himself acted as a healer, bodily and mentally. But more is necessary, namely, the dependence on that which gives ultimate independence, the image of that which includes and transcends all father and mother images, the life of that which makes it possible to hate and to love every life, including our own. No human problem and certainly not the family problem can be solved on a finite level. This is true although we know that even the image of God can be distorted by the images of father and mother, so that its saving power is almost lost. This is the danger of all religion and a serious limit for our religious work. But it is not a limit for God, who again and again breaks through the images we have made of Him, and who has shown in Christ that He is not only father and mother to us, but also child, and that therefore in Him the inescapable conflicts of every family are overcome. The Father who is also child is more than a father as He is more than a child. Therefore we can pray to the Father in heaven without transferring our hostility against the father image to Him. Because God has become child, it is possible for us to say the Our Father.

15

"ALL IS YOURS"

If anyone among you thinks that he is wise in this age, let him become a fool that he may become wise. For the wisdom of this world is folly with God.

I CORINTHIANS 3:18-19.

WHEN A SPEAKER IN A MORNING CHAPEL service used this as his text, I got a written question in class: "What do you think about this morning's sermon?" And this was the implication: How can philosophy stand in view of Paul's depreciating words? I want to answer by trying to interpret what I believe Paul means, not only in the passage above but in the whole context. At the end of his discussion he gives the key by saying: *Let no one boast of men. For all things are yours, whether Paul or Apollos or Cephas or the world or life or death or the present or the future, all are yours; and you are Christ's and Christ is God's.* (I CORINTHIANS 3:21–23.)

Paul has asked, "Has not God made foolish the wisdom of the world?" And now he exclaims, "World and life and Apollos are yours." This means that the wisdom of the world is ours also. How could it be otherwise? We could not even read Paul's words without the wisdom of the world which enables us to understand an-

cient texts, which gives us the technical tools to spread
the Christian message all over the earth, which produces and sustains the political and educational and
artistic institutions which serve and protect the Church.
All this is ours. And even the different theologies are
ours: the more dialectical one of Paul, the more ritual-
istic one of Peter, the more apologetic one of Apollos.
There is only one type of theology which Paul dislikes
—that which wants to monopolize the Christ and call
itself the party of Christ. For each of these theologies
wisdom of the world is needed; scribes are needed, de-
baters are needed, philosophers are needed, a language
is needed to which everybody contributes. It is impossible to deny all this. But it is possible to discredit
through loose talk what one cannot avoid using at the
same time. There is a deep dishonesty in the accusation
against the use of historical research and philosophical
thought in theology. In daily life one calls somebody
dishonest who brings defamation upon those whom he
uses. We should not commit this dishonesty in our theological work. And we cannot escape using the wisdom
of this world. It is no escape if we say: Let us use a
little of it, but not much, in order to escape the dangers implied in it. This certainly is not what Paul means.
The whole world is yours, he says, the whole life, present and future, not parts of it. These important words
speak of scientific knowledge and its passion, artistic
beauty and its excitement, politics and their use of
power, eating and drinking and their joy, sexual love
and its ecstasy, family life and its warmth and friendship with its intimacy, justice with its clarity, nature with
its might and restfulness, the man-made world above

nature, the technical world and its fascination, philosophy with its humility—daring only to call itself love of wisdom—and its profundity—daring to ask ultimate questions. In all of these things is wisdom of this world and power of this world and all these things are ours. They belong to us and we belong to them; we create them and they fulfill us.

But . . . and this "but" of Paul's is not one of those "buts" in which everything is taken back that was given before. The great "but" to the world which is ours gives both the foundation and the limit of the world that is ours: "And you are Christ's," namely, that Christ whose Cross is foolishness and weakness to the wisdom of the world. The wisdom of this world in all its forms cannot know God, and the power of this world with all its means cannot reach God. If they try it, they produce idolatry and are revealed in their foolishness which is the foolishness of idolatry. No finite being can attain the infinite without being broken as He who represented the world, and its wisdom and its power, was broken on the Cross. This is the foolishness and the weakness of the Cross which is ultimate wisdom and which is the reason that Christ is not another bearer of wisdom and power of this world but that He is God's. The Cross makes Him God's. And out of this foolishness we win the wisdom to use what is ours, the wisdom of the world, even philosophy. If it be unbroken, it controls us. If it be broken, it is ours. "Broken" does not mean reduced or emaciated or controlled, but it means undercut in its idolatric claim.

Paul's courage in affirming everything given, his openness towards the world, his sovereignty towards

life should put to shame each of us as well as all our
Churches. We are afraid to accept what is given to us;
we are in compulsive self-seclusion towards our world,
we try to escape life instead of controlling it. We do not
behave as if everything were ours. And the Churches
do so even less. The reason for this is that we and our
Churches do not know as Paul did what it means to
be Christ's and because of being Christ's, to be God's.

16

"IS THERE ANY WORD FROM THE LORD?"

I did not send the prophets, yet they ran; I did not speak to them, yet they prophesied. But if they had stood in my council, then they would have proclaimed my words to my people, and they would have turned them from their evil way, and from the evil of their doings.

Am I a God at hand, says the Lord, and not a God afar off? Can a man hide himself in secret places so that I cannot see him? says the Lord. Do I not fill heaven and earth? says the Lord. I have heard what the prophets have said who prophesy lies in my name, saying, "I have dreamed, I have dreamed!" How long shall there be lies in the heart of the prophets who prophesy lies, and who prophesy the deceit of their own heart, who think to make my people forget my name by their dreams which they tell one another, even as their fathers forgot my name for Baal? Let the prophet who has a dream tell the dream, but let him who has my word speak my word faithfully. What has straw in common with wheat? says the Lord. Is not my word like fire, says the Lord, and like a hammer which breaks the rock in pieces? Therefore, behold, I am against the prophets, says

the Lord, who steal my words from one another.
Behold, I am against the prophets, says the Lord,
who use their tongues and say, "Says the Lord."

JEREMIAH 23:21-31.

*Then Zedekiah the king asked Jeremiah secretly
in his house and said: "Is there any word from the
Lord?" And Jeremiah said: "There is: For thou shalt
be delivered into the hand of the king of Babylon."*

JEREMIAH 37:17.

IS THERE ANY WORD FROM THE LORD?
This is a question asked by men in all periods of history. It has been asked by kings in moments of danger.
They asked it of priests and prophets. It has been asked
by people in all ages and places in times of unrest.
They asked it of extraordinary men and women, often
of those considered to be abnormal, of ecstatics and
hysterics. It has been asked by individuals in moments
of great personal decisions. They asked it of holy Scriptures which should give a special word to them, from
saints and inner voices.

What about ourselves? Have we never asked for a
word from the Lord? Many, certainly, will answer with
a definite "No." They will tell us that they always decided for themselves, using their own reasonable judgment, based on experience, knowledge, and intelligence.
Perhaps they impress us. Perhaps we are ashamed to
confess that sometimes we *have* asked for a word from
the Lord. But let us wait with our answer until we have
found out what these words mean.

We should not be misled by the phrase, "word from the Lord." It sounds as if we turned to a heavenly authority after all others, including the authority of reason, have failed. It sounds as if we asked the Lord of providence to give us for a moment a glimpse into what He plans for us, individually and in history. But such a favor is not granted. The answers given by seers, ecstatics, books and inner voices are mostly ambiguous, open to different interpretations, so that we would have to ask for a second Divine word to interpret the first, and so on indefinitely. Or, these answers are clear and agree with the best wisdom we can have without them. Therefore, I repeat: Let us not be misled by the phrase "word from the Lord." It is not an oracle-word telling us what to do or to expect. Then what is it?

It is the voice from another dimension than that in which we ordinarily live. It cuts into the dimension of things and events which we call our world. It does not help us to manage things within this dimension more successfully than before. It does not add to our knowledge of the factors which influence a situation, it does not remove the responsibility for our decisions. It does something else. It elevates the situation in which we have to decide, into the light of a new dimension, the dimension of that which is ultimately important and infinitely significant and for which we use the word "Divine."

So it was in the case of the king Zedekiah and of the false prophets with whom Jeremiah had to fight. The king came to Jeremiah in a hopeless situation, in a situation into which he had brought himself and his people through guilt and error and disregard of the warnings of the prophet. He was supported in his wrong decision by nationalistic politicians who called themselves "prophets" without having received a word from God. They did not interpret the situation of Judah in the midst of threatening empires in its seriousness. They lacked the realism which is the quality of true prophetism. They were not able to look beyond political chances and military calculations. And so disaster approached and brought about Zedekiah's desperate attempts to get a consoling or helping word from the prophet. But he did not get it. Out of his prison Jeremiah tells him the only thing he did *not* want to hear: You shall be delivered into the hand of the king of Babylon! God will not save you! And the king felt: So it is! He did not slay the prophet of doom, as present-day dictators or nationalistic mobs would do. On the contrary, he helped him out of his miserable prison. But he did not do anything to change the situation. It was too late for this politically and psychologically, and the threat of the prophet, the word he had received from the Lord for Zedekiah, became a terrible reality. Yet it was spoken in vain. It has been remembered ever since, not as an interesting historical report but as an event in which the eternal gives ultimate meaning to an historical catastrophe.

The many words from the Lord which are recorded in the Old Testament have the same quality. They are not promises of an omnipotent ruler replacing political or military strength. They are not lessons handed down by an omniscient teacher, replacing sound judgments. They are not advices of a heavenly counselor, replacing intelligent human counsel. But they are manifesta-

tions of something ultimate breaking into our existence
with all its preliminary concerns and insights. They do
not add something to our situation, but they add a
dimension to the dimension in which we ordinarily live.
The word from the Lord is the word which speaks out
of the depth of our situation. It is, one could say, the
deepest meaning of the situation, of every situation
which comes to us in such words.

It is also the depth of our own situation that speaks
to us when we receive a word from the Lord.

Let us imagine an hour in which we have to make
an important decision, be it the choice of a vocation,
be it the choice of a mate for life. We know most of
the factors which could determine our decision, and
we know the ways our souls work in relation to these
factors. Nevertheless, we cannot decide. *The anxiety
of the possible* makes us restless. We see one, two, perhaps more possibilities. We realize a disturbing number
of possible consequences in each of them. We ask
friends, counsellors; we seek for counsel in ourselves.
But the anxiety of having to decide increases. And a
longing grows in our souls, a longing for something that
liberates us from the anxiety of the possible and gives
us the courage toward the real. It is the question of our
text: Is there a word from the Lord? And perhaps an
answer has been received. But it was not an oracle-
word pointing to the right vocation to choose, or the
right man or woman to join with. It was a voice out
of the depth of our situation, elevating our concrete
problems into an ultimate perspective. In doing so, it
probably has devaluated some factors determining our
decision and has stressed others. Or it has left the bal-

ance of possibilities unchanged, but has given us the courage to make a decision with all the risks of a decision, including error, failure, guilt. The word from the Lord, the voice out of the depth of our situation, ends the anxiety of the possible and gives the courage to affirm the real with its many questionable elements.

Some of you may say: If this is what "word from the Lord" means, how can it help me in moments of decision? But would you really want me to tell you where to turn for an oracle which would liberate you from the burden of decision? Certainly, that which is weak in you would like it. But that which is strong in you would reject it. The Lord from whom you derive a word wants you to decide for yourselves. He does not offer you a safe way. You may be wrong in your decision. But if you realize that in relation to God man is always wrong, your wrong may turn out to be right. If in the presence of the eternal you risk defeat, through your very defeat a word from the Lord has come to you.

Let us now look at a quite different situation, one in which we do not have to make a great decision, and in which the small decisions we have to make daily do not give us much anxiety. There are not concrete threats against life and well-being, there is not a depressing guilt feeling or a despair about ourselves. There is not a disintegrating doubt or an intolerable emptiness. There is not an extreme situation. Does this mean that there is no desire to ask for a word from the Lord? Are the situations which are not extreme situations, deprived of a word out of the dimension of the eternal? Is God silent if the foundations of our existence are *not* shaken? A hard question, and answered in many different ways!

How would we answer? I shall never forget the word of a wise old man who said to my grandfather when I was still a child, "I need somebody whom I can thank when a great joy is given to me." Can we share this experience? Do we remember such moments in which the eternal made itself felt to us through the abundance or greatness or beauty of the temporal? I believe that none of us is completely without such experiences. But did we not say that a word from the Lord is the eternal cutting into the temporal? Certainly that is what it is! But cutting into the temporal does not mean negating it. This it *can* mean, and this it *does* mean whenever we are driven into an ultimate situation. There are in everybody's life such situations, and they are frequent in man's tragic history. But the eternal can also cut into the temporal by affirming it, by elevating a piece of it out of the ordinary context of temporal things and events, making it translucent for the Divine glory. Without such moments, life would be poor and sad; there would be no creations in which the greatness of life is expressed. But they exist, and the eternal shines through them; they can become a word from the Lord to us.

But still some of you are thinking: All this may be as you say, but it remains strange to us. Neither in ultimate situations nor in moments of a great elevation has the eternal cut into our temporal existence. We never got a word from the Lord. Maybe you did not hear it. But certainly it was spoken to you. For there is always a word from the Lord, a word that *has* been spoken. The problem of man is not that God does not speak to him: God *does* speak to everyone who has a human countenance. For this is what makes him man. He who is not able to perceive something ultimate, something infinitely significant, is not a man. Man is man because he is able to receive a word from the dimension of the eternal. The question is not that mankind has not received any word from the Lord; the question is that it has been received and resisted and distorted. This is the predicament of all of us. Human existence is never without that which breaks vertically into it. Man is never without a manifestation of that which is ultimately serious and infinitely meaningful. He is never without a word from the Lord and he never ceases resisting and distorting it, both when he has to hear it and when he has to say it.

Every Christian, and especially every Christian minister, should be aware of this: We resist and distort the word from the Lord not only when we hear it, but also when we say it. When we ask why our message of the Word of God is rejected, we often find that one does not reject that for which we stand, but the *way* in which we stand for it. Many of those who reject the Word of God reject it because the way we say it is utterly meaningless to them. They know the dimension of the eternal, but they cannot accept our names for it. If we cling to their words, we may doubt whether they have received a word from the Lord. If we meet them as persons, we know they have.

There is always a word from the Lord, a word that has been spoken. The Christian Church believes that this word has a central content, and that it has the name Jesus the Christ. Therefore, the Church calls not His *words* but His *Being* the Word of God. The Church believes that in His Being, the eternal has broken into the temporal in a way which once for all gives us *a* word, nay, *the* word from the Lord. It believes that whatever word from the Lord has been said in all history and in every individual life, is implied in this Word, which is not words but reality, a new reality, the reality of the eternal in the temporal, conquering the resistance and the distortions of the temporal.

So we have not *a*, but *the* word from the Lord? As Christians we can boast that we have it? Can we really? Did we not receive the message through men, and are not we who heard it men? And does that not mean that the message, while it went through the mouths of those who said it and through the ears of us who heard it, lost its power to cut into our world and our soul?

Those who said it—the Church and its servants in all periods—made it a matter of law and tradition, of habit and convention. They made it into something we believe we know and have tried to follow. It does not cut any more into our ordinary world. It has become a part of our ordinary world. Like the prophets with whom Jeremiah fights in our text, the ministers of the word have ceased to ask, to cry for, a word from the Lord. They claim to have it as their possession, and since the Word of God can never be a possession, the words they say are not a word from the Lord. We have received it. But as it has been distorted in the mouths of the preachers, so it has been resisted in the ears of the listeners, that is, in all of us. We hear it, but we cannot perceive it. As Christians we do not reject it, but it has lost its voice, that voice with which Jahweh spoke into the hearts of the prophets, that voice with which the Spirit spoke into the hearts of the disciples. We hear the words which have been said before. But we do not feel that they speak *to* our situation, and *out of* the depth of our situation. They may even produce torturing doubts and drive us to ask passionately for a word from the Lord *against* what we have received as the Word of God, in Bible and Church.

For there is no word from the Lord except the word which is spoken now. How can we get such a word that is spoken now and is spoken to us?

There is only one answer: By keeping ourselves open when it comes to us! This is not easy. We try to resist it, and if it is too strong for us we try to falsify it. We may be in a situation out of which we cannot extricate ourselves. It is too late for this. So the word from the Lord comes as a word of judgment and we cannot take it. Or the word which comes to us requests a radical change in our ways of life and thought. But this we cannot achieve, and we back into our habits of good and evil, of right and wrong. Or we are in doubt and guilt and despair, and the word comes to us and tells us that we can say yes to ourselves because an eternal yes has been said to us and of us. But we resist the word which demands of us the courage to say yes to ourselves because we are in love with our doubt and our guilt and our despair.

It is not easy to keep oneself open for a word from the Lord. And nobody can make it easier for us by giving us the direction in which to listen. No fixed place can be named, either in our religious tradition or in our cultural creations, or in the depth of our souls. But for this very reason, no place is excluded from communicating to us a word from the Lord. It is always present and tries always to be perceived by us. It is like the air, surrounding us, omnipresent, trying to enter every empty space. It is the empty space in our souls into which it tries to enter here and now. So the last question is: Is there an empty space in *your* soul? Or is everything filled with that which is transitory, preliminary, ultimately insignificant, however important it tries to be? Without a soul opened for it, no word from the Lord can be received. Listening with an open soul, keeping an empty space in our inner life, sharpening our spiritual hearing: this is the only thing we can do. But this is much. And blessed are those whose minds and hearts are open.

Therefore, let us keep open our ears and let us keep open our hearts, and ask with great seriousness and great passion: Is there a word from the Lord, a word for me, here and now, a word for our world in this moment? It *is* there, it tries to come to you. Keep open for it!

17

SEEING AND HEARING

Jesus said, "For judgment I came into this world, that those who do not see may see, and that those who see may become blind." Some of the Pharisees near him heard this, and they said to him, "Are we also blind?" Jesus said to them, "If you were blind, you would have no guilt; but now that you say, 'We see,' your guilt remains."

JOHN 9:39-41.

THE BIBLE OF BOTH TESTAMENTS, LIKE much other religious literature, speaks again and again of "seeing." "Come and see." These words of the disciple sound through the writings of prophets and apostles. We *have* seen: this is the message of Gospels and Epistles. It is not true that religious faith is belief in things without evidence. The word "evidence" means "seeing thoroughly." And we are asked to *see*. We have present with us what we see; therefore, we want to see what we love, what is significant for us. The great men of God wanted to see God; Moses asked this as the highest of all favors of Jahveh. Isaiah was made the most powerful of the prophets after he had seen God in the temple. Jesus blesses the pure in heart as those

125

who will see God. In the Fourth Gospel He says about Himself that He has seen the Father, and that whoever has seen Him has also seen the Father. In pious imagery the angels and the saints are described as those who see God face to face. And the ultimate fulfillment, the end of all moving and striving, is pictured as the eternal vision of God.

But doubts and questions arise when we look at our present human predicament. Is faith not the opposite of vision? Must we not believe without seeing? Does Jesus not bless those who have not seen and yet believe? Is not faith defined as the evidence of things not seen? And does not Paul write, "We walk by faith, not by sight"? "We look not at the things which are seen, but at the things which are not seen. For the things which are seen are temporal, but the things which are not seen are eternal"? All this seems to indicate that faith must be based on *hearing* and not on seeing. You *hear* about something you do not see. You believe him who tells you. You accept the word of the authorities in humility and obedience. You believe what the Bible says because the Bible says it. You accept what the Church teaches because it is taught by the Church. You call the word of the Bible and of the Church "Word of God." You hear, you believe, you obey, but you do not see.

In former centuries there was a long-lasting struggle in the Church about the religious significance of hearing and seeing. First, seeing prevailed, but then hearing became more and more significant. Finally, in the days of the Reformation hearing became completely victorious. The typical Protestant church-buildings bear witness to this victory. They are halls to hear sermons, emptied of everything to be seen of pictures and sculptures, of lights and stained windows, of most of the sacramental activities. Around the desk of the preacher a room was built to listen to the words of the law and the gospel. The eye could not find a place to rest in contemplation. Hearing replaced seeing, obedience replaced vision.

But Jesus says, "I came into this world, that those who do not see may *see*." And the apostle says, "That which we have *seen with our eyes,* which we have looked upon—we proclaim to you." Both speak not about the future, but about something they *have* seen and *still* see. And they certainly do not feel as do old and new theologians that there is a conflict between seeing and hearing, between seeing and believing. "That which we have seen *and* heard," writes the apostle. "Everyone who *sees* the Son and *believes* in Him," says Jesus. And most important and surprising: That which we have seen with our eyes according to our gospel is the Word, the eternal Word or Logos in whom God speaks, who can be seen through the works of creation and who is visible in the man Jesus. The Word can be *seen,* this is the highest unity of hearing and seeing, that is the truth which can bridge the Protestant and the Catholic half-truths.

Seeing is the most astonishing of our natural powers. It receives the light, the first of all that is created, and as the light does it conquers darkness and chaos. It creates for us an ordered world, things distinguished from each other and from us. Seeing shows us their unique countenance and the larger whole to which they belong. Wherever we see, a piece of the original chaos is transformed into creation. We distinguish, we recognize, we give a name, we know. "I have seen"—that means in Greek "I know." From seeing, all science starts, to seeing it must always return. We want to ask those who have seen with their eyes and we ourselves want to see with our eyes. Only the human eye is able to see in this way, to see a world in every small thing and to see a universe *of* all things. Therefore the human eye is infinite in reach and irresistible in power. It is the correlate to the light of creation.

But seeing means more than the creation of a world. Where we see we unite with what we see. Seeing is a kind of union. As poetry has described it, we *drink* colors and forms, forces and expressions. They become a part of ourselves. They give abundance to the poverty of our loneliness. Even when we are unaware of them they stream into us; but sometimes we notice them and welcome them and desire more of them.

Not all seeing has this character of union. If we look at things and observe them merely to control and to use them, no real union takes place. We keep them at a distance. We try to bring them into our power, to use them for our purposes, as means for our ends. There is no love in this kind of seeing. We glimpse the beings that shall serve us coldly; we have for those which we use a look, curious or indifferent, sensational or aggressive, hostile or cruel. There is abuse in the looking at those which we *use*. It is a seeing that violates and separates. This is the look of the masses who in medieval paintings are looking at the Crucified. But even this kind of seeing creates some union, though union through separation. But the seeing that really unites is different. Our language has a word for it: Intuition. This means seeing *into*. It is an intimate seeing, a grasping and being grasped. It is a seeing shaped by love. Plato, the teacher of the centuries, whose visions and words have deeply influenced the Fourth Gospel and the Church, knew about the seeing which unites. He called the love which drives us to a genuine intuition the "child of poverty and abundance." It is the love which fills our want with the abundance of our world. But it fills us in such a way that the disrupted multitude is not the last we see—a view which disrupts ourselves. The last we see lies in that which unites, which is eternal *in* and *above* the transitory things. Into this view Plato wanted to initiate his followers.

This leads us to another characteristic of seeing, the most significant of all. We never see only what we see; we always see something else with it and through it! Seeing creates, seeing unites, and above all seeing goes beyond itself. If we look at a stone we see directly only the colors and forms of the side which is turned towards us. But with and through this limited surface we are aware of the roundness, of the extension and mass of the structure of the whole thing. We see beyond what we see. If we look at an animal we see directly the colors and forms of its skin. But with it and through it we are aware of the tension and power of its muscles, of its inner strivings which are covered as well as revealed by the skin. We see not color spots, but a living being. If we look at a human face, we see lines and shades, but with it and through it we see a unique, in-comparable personality whose expressions are visible in his face, whose character and destiny have left traces which we understand and in which we can even read something of his future. With and through colors and forms and movements we see friendliness and coldness, hostility and devotion, anger and love, sadness and joy. We see infinitely more than we see when we look into a human face. And we see even beyond this into a new depth. Again the language gives us a help when it speaks of con- templation. Con- templation means going into the temple, into the sphere of the holy, into the deep roots of things, into their creative ground. We see the mysterious powers which we call beauty and truth and goodness. We cannot see them as such, we can see them only in things and events. We see them with and through the shape of a rose and the movements of the stars and the image of a friend. We *can* see them, but it is not *necessary* that we see them. We can close our eyes, we can become blind. Some are blind to any beauty which is more than a pleasant feeling, some are blind to any truth which is more than correct observation and calculation, some are blind to any goodness which is more than usefulness. And some are blind to any ground which is the unity of these powers and which we call "holy." It is the ultimate, the last which we can see with and through all things; and therefore it is the end of all seeing. It is the light itself and therefore it is darkness for our eyes. Only "with and through" can we see it, through things and men, through events and images. This seeing and

not seeing at the same time is what we call faith. Nobody can see God; but we can see him "with and
through." Here the conflict ends between seeing and
hearing. The word tells us where to see and when we
have seen we pronounce what we have seen *and* heard.
In the state which we call faith, sound and vision are
united and perhaps this is the reason why the "holy"
likes to be expressed in music more than in any other
medium. Music gives wings to both, word and image,
and goes beyond both of them.

But for a second time we are called down from the
flight above to the lowliness of our human situation. Our
Gospel calls us blind, all of us. And Jesus says that we
are blind because we believe we see and do not know
that we are blind; and He threatens that we shall be
thrown into more blindness if we insist that we are
seeing. The question is: Where of all places can and
shall we see into the ground of all Being? Who can
lead our contemplation into the temple, into the holy
itself?

Seeing gives us a "world," the order and unity of the
many. But we see within this order, disorder; within
the unity, conflict threatening to explode the world
itself and to bring back the old darkness of the chaos.
And order and chaos are so mixed with each other that
we often feel dizzy, without ground and meaning, de-
siring to keep our eyes closed. Seeing unites us with
what we see. But we see so many things and beings
with which we do not want to be united, towards which
we are indifferent or hostile, which are indifferent or
hostile to us, which are repulsive and which we hate

to see just *because* every seeing unites, even if it is
through hate. And it may be even our own self that
we do not want to see because we are repelled by our
image and because we hate it if we see it. Not in love
but in hate are we united with ourselves, and perhaps
we want to deprive ourselves of our eyes like Œdipus,
of our eyes which first did not see what they ought to
see and now cannot stand to see what they must see.
And is not that which we love to see and that which
we hate to see so mixed that we often praise the poverty of not seeing? Seeing is seeing with and through
beings into their depth, into the good and the true and
into their holy ground. But which are the beings and
images that shall lead us to this temple? Those whom
Jesus called blind believed they knew the way to the
temple, to the holy and the holiest. Innumerable temples all over the world contain things and images with
and through which we can see God. But what we see
are idols, fascinating, horrible, overwhelming in seductive beauty or destructive power, demanding what cannot be fulfilled, promising what cannot be given, giving what elevates and lowers at the same time. And this
is so because they hold us fast to themselves and do
not lead us beyond. Our eyes are bound by them, often
bound by the demonic fascination they exercise and
with which they take possession of us. We contemplate
them, we go into their temples, we unite with them in
self-surrender, and we leave them emptied, despairing,
destroyed. This is the great temptation of seeing. This
is the reason why hearing was put against seeing. It
is the reason why images were destroyed again and

again and every image forbidden, why the temples were burned and God was called the Infinite Void. But this cannot be the last word. Emptiness can be both light and darkness; and we want light, the light which is life and vision.

Jesus also could have become an idol, a national and religious hero, fascinating and destructive. This is what the disciples and the masses wanted Him to be. They saw Him, they loved Him, they saw with and through Him the good and the true, the holy itself. But they succumbed to the temptation of seeing. They kept to that which must be sacrificed if God shall be seen with and through any mortal being. And when He sacrificed Himself, they looked away in despair like those whose image and idol is destroyed. But He was too strong; He drew their eyes back to Him, but now to Him crucified. And they could stand it, for they saw with Him and through Him the God who is really God. He who has seen Him has seen the Father: This is true only of the Crucified. But of Him it *is* true. Certainly He is not the only one to look at in intuition and contemplation. We are not asked to stare at Him, as some do. We are not asked to look away from everything for His sake, as some do. We are not asked to give up the abundance of His creation as some do. We are not asked to refuse union with what we see as some do. But we are asked to see with and through everything into the depth into which He shows the way. We shall see into it unimpeded by that which tries to keep us, away from the last depth. And when we are tired of seeing the abundance of the world with all its disorder, its hate and separation, its demonic destruction, and if we are also unable to look into the blinding light of the divine ground, then let us close our eyes. And then it might happen that we see the picture of someone who looks at us with eyes of infinite human depth and therefore of divine power and love. And these eyes say to us "Come and see."

18

THE PARADOX OF PRAYER

Likewise the Spirit helps us in our weakness; for we do not know how to pray as we ought, but the Spirit himself intercedes for us with sighs too deep for words. And he who searches the hearts of men knows what is the mind of the Spirit, because the Spirit intercedes for the saints according to the will of God.

ROMANS 8:26-27.

THIS PASSAGE OF ROMANS ABOUT THE Spirit interceding for us "with sighs too deep for words" belongs to the most mysterious of Paul's sayings. It expresses the experience of a man who knew how to pray and who, because he knew how to pray, said that he did *not* know how to pray. Perhaps we may draw from this confession of the apostle the conclusion that those amongst us who act as if they knew how to pray, do not know how at all. For this conclusion we could find much evidence in our daily experience. Ministers are used to praying publicly on all kinds of occasions, some of which offer themselves naturally to a prayer, others only artificially and against good taste. It is not unimportant to know the right hour for praying and the right hour for not praying. This is a warning, on the periphery of what Paul wants to say, but a necessary

warning, especially to ministers and laymen who are
leaders in the Church.

The next step leads us nearer to the center of Paul's
problem: There are two main types of prayer, the fixed
liturgical and the free spontaneous prayer. Both of them
show the truth of Paul's assertion, that we do not know
"to pray as we ought." The liturgical prayer often becomes mechanical or incomprehensible or both. The
history of the Church has shown that this was the fate
even of the Lord's Prayer. Paul certainly knew the "Our
Father" when he wrote that we do not know how to
pray. It does not prove that we know how to pray when
we make a liturgical law out of the example of praying
which Jesus gave to his disciples.

But if we turn from the formulated to the spontaneous prayer, we are not better off. Very often the spontaneous prayer is an ordinary conversation with somebody who is called "God," but who is actually another
man to whom we tell things, often at great length, to
whom we give thanks and of whom we ask favors. This
certainly does not prove that we know how to pray.

The liturgical Churches which use classical formulas
should ask themselves whether they do not prevent the
people of *our* time from praying as they honestly can.
And the non-liturgical Churches who give the freedom
to make up prayers at any moment, should ask themselves whether they do not profane prayer and deprive
it of its mystery.

And now let us take a third step, into the center of
Paul's thought. Whether at the right time or not,
whether a formulated or a spontaneous prayer, the question is decisive whether a prayer is possible at all. Ac-

cording to Paul, it is humanly impossible. This we should never forget when we pray: We do something humanly impossible. We talk to somebody who is not somebody else, but who is nearer to us than we ourselves are. We address somebody who can never become an object of our address because he is always subject, always acting, always creating. We tell something to Him who knows not only what we tell Him but also all the unconscious tendencies out of which our conscious words grow. This is the reason why prayer is humanly impossible. Out of this insight Paul gives a mysterious solution to the question of the right prayer: It is God Himself who prays through us, when we pray to Him. God Himself in us: that is what Spirit means. Spirit is another word for "God present," with shaking, inspiring, transforming power. Something in us, which is not we ourselves, intercedes before God for us. We cannot bridge the gap between God and ourselves even through the most intensive and frequent prayers; the gap between God and ourselves can be bridged only by God. And so Paul gives us the surprising picture of God interceding for us before Himself. Such symbols—like all symbols concerning God—are absurd if taken literally. They are profound if taken as genuine symbols. The symbol of God interceding before Himself for us says that God knows more about us than that of which we are conscious. He "searches the hearts of men." These are words which anticipate the present-day insight, of which we are rightly proud, that the small light of consciousness rises on a large basis of unconscious drives and images. But if this is so, who else can bring our whole being before God except God

Himself, who alone knows the deep things in our soul?

This may help us also to understand the most mysterious part of Paul's description of prayer, namely, that the Spirit "intercedes with sighs too deep for words." Just because every prayer is humanly impossible, just because it brings deeper levels of our being before God than the level of consciousness, something happens in it that cannot be expressed in words. Words, created *by* and used *in* our conscious life, are not the essence of prayer. The essence of prayer is the act of God who is working in us and raises our whole being to Himself. The way in which this happens is called by Paul "sighing." Sighing is an expression of the weakness of our creaturely existence. Only in terms of wordless sighs can we approach God, and even these sighs are His work in us.

This finally answers a question often asked by Christians: Which kind of prayer is most adequate to our relation to God? The prayer in which we thank or the prayer in which we beg, the prayer of intercession or of confession or of praise? Paul does not make these distinctions. They are dependent on words; but the sighing of the Spirit in us is too deep for words and for the distinction of kinds of prayer. The Spiritual prayer is elevation to God in the power of God and it includes all forms of prayer.

A last word to those who feel that they cannot find the words of prayer and remain silent towards God. This may be lack of Spirit. It also may be that their silence is silent *prayer,* namely, the sighs which are too deep for words. Then He who searches the hearts of men, knows and hears.

PART III

The New Being as Fulfillment

19

THE MEANING OF JOY

When the Lord restored the fortunes of Zion, we were like those who dream. Then our mouth was filled with laughter, and our tongue with shouts of joy; then they said among the nations, "The Lord has done great things for them." The Lord had done great things for us; we are glad.

Restore our fortunes, O Lord, like the watercourses in the Negeb! May those who sow in tears reap with shouts of joy! He that goes forth weeping, bearing the seed for sowing, shall come home with shouts of joy, bringing his sheaves with him.

PSALM 126.

Truly, truly, I say to you, you will weep and lament, but the world will rejoice; you will be sorrowful, but your sorrow will turn into joy. When a woman is in travail she has sorrow, because her hour has come; but when she is delivered of the child, she no longer remembers the anguish, for joy that a child is born into the world. So you have sorrow now, but I will see you again and your hearts will rejoice, and no one will take your joy from you.

JOHN 16:20-22.

141

These things I have spoken to you, that my joy may be in you, and that your joy may be full.

JOHN 15:11.

THE BIBLE ABOUNDS IN ADMONITIONS to rejoice. Paul's word to the Philippians, "again I will say, Rejoice," represents an ever-present element in Biblical religion. For the men of the Old and New Testaments the lack of joy is a consequence of man's separation from God, and the presence of joy is a consequence of the reunion with God.

Joy is demanded, and it can be given. It is not a thing one simply has. It is not easy to attain. It is and always was a rare and precious thing. And it has always been a difficult problem among Christians. Christians are accused of destroying the joy of life, this natural endowment of every creature. The greatest of the modern foes of Christianity, Friedrich Nietzsche, himself the son of a Protestant minister, has expressed his judgment about Jesus in the words, "His disciples should look more redeemed." We should subject ourselves to the piercing force of these words and should ask ourselves, "Is our lack of joy due to the fact that we are Christians, or to the fact that we are not sufficiently Christian?" Perhaps we can defend ourselves convincingly against the criticism that we are people who despise life, whose behavior is a permanent accusation of life. Perhaps we can show that this is a distortion of the truth.

But let us be honest. Is there not enough foundation for criticism? Are not many Christians—ministers, students of theology, evangelists, missionaries, Christian educators and social workers, pious laymen and lay-women, even the children of such parents—surrounded by an air of heaviness, of oppressive sternness, of lack of humor and irony about themselves? We cannot deny this. Our critics outside the Church are right. And we ourselves should be even more critical than they, but critical on a deeper level.

As Christians we know our inner conflicts about accepting or rejecting joy. We are suspicious of the gifts of nature which contribute to joy, because we are suspicious of nature itself, although we confess that it is Divine creation, knowing what God has spoken about His creation: "Behold, it was very good!" We are suspicious of the creations of culture which contribute to joy because we are suspicious of man's creativity, although we confess that God has commanded man to cultivate the garden of the earth which He has made subject to him. And even if we overcome our suspicions and affirm and accept the gifts of nature and the creations of culture, we often do so with an uneasy conscience. We know that we *should* be free for joy, that as Paul says, "all is ours," but our courage is inferior to our knowledge. We do not dare to affirm our world and ourselves; and if we dare to, in a moment of courage, we try to atone for it by self-reproaches and self-punishments, and we draw upon ourselves malicious criticism by those who never have dared. Therefore, many Christians try to compromise. They try to hide their feeling of joy, or they try to avoid joys which are too intense, in order to avoid self-accusations which are too harsh. Such an experience of the suppression of joy, and guilt about joy in Christian groups, almost drove me to a break with Christianity. What passes for joy in these groups is an emaciated, intentionally childish, unexciting, unecstatic thing, without color and danger, without heights and depths.

It is difficult to deny that this is the state of things in many Christian churches. But now we hear the question from both the Christian and the non-Christian sides: "Is not joy, as observed in the Bible, something completely different from the joy of life, which is lacking in many Christians? Do not the Psalmist and Paul and the Jesus of the Fourth Gospel speak of a joy which transcends the natural joy of life? Do they not speak about the joy in God? Is not the decision to be a Christian a decision for the joy in God instead of for the joy of life?"

The first and simplest answer to these questions is that life is God's, and God is the creative Ground of life. He is infinitely more than any life process. But He works creatively through all of them. Therefore, no conflict is necessary between the joy in God and the joy of life. But this first answer, great and joyful as it is, is not sufficient; for "joy of life" can mean many things.

Joy seems to be the opposite of pain. But we know that pain and joy can exist together. Not joy but pleasure is the opposite of pain. There are people who believe that man's life is a continuous flight from pain and a persistent search for pleasure. I have never seen a human being of whom that is true. It is true only of beings who have lost their humanity, either through complete disintegration or through mental illness. The ordinary human being is able to sacrifice pleasures and to take pain upon himself for a cause, for somebody or something he loves and deems worthy of pain and sacrifice. He can disregard both pain and pleasure because he is directed *not* towards his pleasure but towards the things he loves and with which he wants to unite. If we desire something because of the pleasure we may get out of it, we may get the pleasure but we shall not get joy. If we try to find someone through whom we may get pleasure, we may get pleasure but we shall not have joy. If we search for something in order to avoid pain, we may avoid pain, but we shall not avoid sorrow. If we try to use someone to protect us from pain, he may protect us from pain but he will not protect us from sorrow. Pleasures *can* be provided and pain *can* be avoided, if we use or abuse other beings. But joy cannot be attained and sorrow cannot be overcome in this way. Joy is possible only when we are driven towards things and persons because of what they are and not because of what we can get from them. The joy about our work is spoiled when we perform it not because of what we produce but because of the pleasures with which it can provide us, or the pain against which it can protect us. The pleasure about the fact that *I* am successful spoils the joy about the success itself. Our joy about knowing truth and experiencing beauty is spoiled if we enjoy not the truth and the beauty but the fact that it is *I* who enjoys them.

Power can give joy only if it is free from the pleasure about having power and if it is a method of creating something worthwhile. Love relations, most conspicuously relations between the sexes, remain without joy if we use the other one as a means for pleasure or as a means to escape pain. This is a threat to all human relations. It is not an external law which warns us about certain forms of these relations, but the wisdom born out of past experiences which tells us that some of these relations may give pleasure, but that they do not give joy. They do not give joy because they do not fulfill what we are, and that for which we strive. Every human relation is joyless in which the other person is not sought because of what he is in himself, but because of the pleasure he can give us and the pain from which he can protect us.

To seek pleasure for the sake of pleasure is to avoid reality, the reality of other beings and the reality of ourselves. But only the fulfillment of what we really are can give us joy. Joy is nothing else than the awareness of our being fulfilled in our true being, in our personal center. And this fulfillment is possible only if we unite ourselves with what others really are. It is reality that gives joy, and reality alone. The Bible speaks so often of joy because it is the most realistic of all books. "Rejoice!" That means: "Penetrate from what *seems* to be real to that which is *really* real." Mere pleasure, in yourselves and in all other beings, remains in the realm of illusion about reality. Joy is born out of union with reality itself.

One of the roots of the desire for pleasure is the feeling of emptiness and the pain of boredom following from it. Emptiness is the lack of relatedness to things and persons and meanings; it is even the lack of being related to oneself. Therefore we try to escape from ourselves and the loneliness of ourselves, but we do not reach the others and their world in a genuine relation.

And so we use them for a kind of pleasure which can be called "fun." But it is not the creative kind of fun often connected with play; it is, rather, a shallow, distracting, greedy way of "having fun." And it is not by chance that it is that type of fun which can easily be commercialized, for it is dependent on calculable reactions, without passion, without risk, without love. Of all the dangers that threaten our civilization, this is one of the most dangerous ones: the escape from one's emptiness through a "fun" which makes joy impossible.

Rejoice! This Biblical exhortation is more needed for those who have much "fun" and pleasure than for those who have little pleasure and much pain. It is often easier to unite pain and joy than to unite fun and joy.

Does the Biblical demand for joy prohibit pleasure? Do joy and pleasure exclude each other? By no means! The fulfillment of the center of our being does not exclude partial and peripheral fulfillments. And we must say this with the same emphasis with which we have contrasted joy and pleasure. We must challenge not only those who seek pleasure for pleasure's sake, but also those who reject pleasure because it is pleasure. Man enjoys eating and drinking, beyond the mere animal need of them. It is a partial ever-repeated fulfillment of his striving for life; therefore, it is pleasure and gives joy of life. Man enjoys playing and dancing, the beauty of nature, and the ecstasy of love. They fulfill some of his most intensive strivings for life; therefore, they are pleasure and give joy of life. Man enjoys the power of knowledge and the fascination of art. They fulfill some of his highest strivings for life; therefore, they are pleasure and give joy of life. Man enjoys the community of men in family, friendship, and the social group. They fulfill some fundamental strivings for life; therefore, they are pleasure and give joy of life.

Yet in all these relations the question arises: Is our way of having these pleasures right or wrong? Do we use them for pleasure's sake or because we want to unite in love with all that to which we belong? We never know with certainty. And those of us together with those in the past history of Christianity who have an anxious conscience, prefer to renounce pleasures although they are established as good by creation itself. They hide their anxiety behind parental or social or ecclesiastical prohibitions, calling these prohibitions Divine commands. They justify their fear to affirm the joy of life by appealing to their conscience, calling it the voice of God, or to the need of discipline and self-control, and selflessness, calling them the "imitation of Christ." But Jesus, in contrast to John the Baptist, was called a glutton and a drunkard by His critics. In all these warnings against pleasure, truth is mixed with untruth. Insofar as they strengthen our responsibility, they are true; insofar as they undercut our joy, they are wrong. Therefore let me give another criterion for accepting or rejecting pleasures, the criterion indicated in our text: Those pleasures are good which go together with joy; those are bad which prevent joy. In the light of this norm we should risk the affirmation of pleasures, even if our risk may prove to have been an error. It is not more Christian to reject than to accept pleasure. Let us not forget that the rejection implies a rejection of creation, or as the Church Fathers called it, a blasphemy of the Creator-God. And every Christian should be aware of a fact of which many non-Christians are keenly aware: the suppression of the joy of life produces hatred of life, hidden or open. It can lead to a self-destruction, as many physical and mental diseases prove.

Joy is more than pleasure; and it is more than happiness. Happiness is a state of mind which lasts for a longer or shorter time and is dependent on many conditions, external and internal. In the ancient view it is a gift of the gods which they give and take away again. In the American Constitution, "the pursuit of happiness" is a basic human right. In economic theory the greatest happiness of the greatest possible number of people is the purpose of human action. In the fairy tale, "they lived happily ever after." Happiness can stand a large amount of pain and lack of pleasure. But happiness cannot stand the lack of joy. For joy is the expression of our essential and central fulfillment. No peripheral fulfillments and no favorable conditions can be substituted for the central fulfillment. Even in an unhappy state a great joy can transform unhappiness into happiness. What, then, is this joy?

Let us first ask what is its opposite. It is sorrow. Sorrow is the feeling that we are deprived of our central fulfillment, by being deprived of something that belongs to us and is necessary to our fulfillment. We may be deprived of relatives and friends nearest to us, of a creative work and a supporting community which gave us a meaning of life, of our home, of honor, of love, of bodily or mental health, of the unity of our person, of a good conscience. All this brings sorrow in manifold forms, the sorrow of sadness, the sorrow of loneliness, the sorrow of depression, the sorrow of self-accusation. But it is precisely this kind of situation in which Jesus tells his disciples that His joy shall be with them and that their joy shall be full. For, as Paul calls it, sorrow can be the "sorrow of the world" which ends in the death of final despair, and it can be Divine sorrow which leads to transformation and joy. For joy has something within itself which is beyond joy and sorrow. This something is called blessedness.

Blessedness is the eternal element in joy, that which makes it possible for joy to include in itself the sorrow out of which it arises, and which it takes into itself. In the Beatitudes, Jesus calls the poor, those who mourn, those who hunger and thirst, those who are persecuted, "blessed." And He says to them: "Rejoice and be glad!" Joy within sorrow is possible to those who are blessed, to those in whom joy has the dimension of the eternal.

Here we must once more reply to those who attack Christianity because they believe that it destroys the joy of life. In view of the Beatitudes they say that Christianity undercuts the joy of *this* life by pointing to and preparing for another life. They even challenge the blessedness in the promised life as a refined form of seeking for pleasure in the future life. Again we must confess that in many Christians, joy in this way is postponed till after death, and that there are Biblical words which seem to support this answer. Nevertheless, it is wrong. Jesus will give His joy to His disciples *now*. They shall get it after He has left them, which means in *this* life. And Paul asks the Philippians to have joy *now*. This cannot be otherwise, for blessedness is the expression of God's eternal fulfillment. Blessed are those who participate in this fulfillment here and now. Certainly eternal fulfillment must be seen not only as eternal which is present, but also as eternal which is future. But if it is not seen in the present, it cannot be seen at all.

This joy which has in itself the depth of blessedness is asked for and promised in the Bible. It preserves in itself its opposite, sorrow. It provides the foundation for happiness and pleasure. It is present in all levels of man's striving for fulfillment. It consecrates and directs them. It does not diminish or weaken them. It does not take away the risks and dangers of the joy of life. It makes the joy of life possible in pleasure and pain, in happiness and unhappiness, in ecstasy and sorrow. Where there is joy, there is fulfillment. And where there is fulfillment, there is joy. In fulfillment and joy the inner aim of life, the meaning of creation, and the end of salvation, are attained.

20

OUR ULTIMATE CONCERN

Now as they went on their way, he entered a village; and a woman named Martha received him into her house. And she had a sister called Mary, who sat at the Lord's feet and listened to his teaching. But Martha was distracted with much serving; and she went to him and said, "Lord, do you not care that my sister has left me to serve alone? Tell her then to help me." But the Lord answered, "Martha, Martha, you are anxious and troubled about many things; one thing is needful. Mary has chosen the good portion, which shall not be taken away from her."

LUKE 10:38-42

THE WORDS JESUS SPEAKS TO MARTHA belong to the most famous of all the words in the Bible. Martha and Mary have become symbols for two possible attitudes towards life, for two forces in man and in mankind as a whole, for two kinds of concern. Martha is concerned about many things, but all of them are finite, preliminary, transitory. Mary is concerned about one thing, which is infinite, ultimate, lasting.

Martha's way is not contemptible. On the contrary,

it is the way which keeps the world running. It is the driving force which preserves and enriches life and culture. Without it Jesus could not have talked to Mary and Mary could not have listened to Jesus. Once I heard a sermon dedicated to the justification and glorification of Martha. This can be done. There are innumerable concerns in our lives and in human life generally which demand attention, devotion, passion. But they do not demand *infinite* attention, *unconditional* devotion, *ultimate* passion. They are important, often very important for you and for me and for the whole of mankind. But they are not *ultimately* important. And therefore Jesus praises not Martha, but Mary. She has chosen the right thing, the one thing man needs, the only thing of ultimate concern for every man.

The hour of a church service and every hour of meditative reading is dedicated to listening in the way Mary listened. Something is being said to us, to the speaker as well as to the listeners, something about which we may become infinitely concerned. This is the meaning of every sermon. It shall awaken infinite concern.

What does it mean to be concerned about something? It means that we are involved in it, that a part of ourselves is in it, that we participate with our hearts. And it means even more than that. It points to the way in which we are involved, namely, *anxiously*. The wisdom of our language often identifies concern with anxiety. Wherever we are involved we feel anxiety. There are many things which interest us, which provoke our compassion or horror. But they are not our real concern; they do not produce this driving, torturing anxiety which is present when we are genuinely and seriously concerned. In our story, Martha was seriously concerned. Let us try to remember what gives us concern in the course of an average day, from the moment of awakening to the last moment before falling asleep, and even beyond that. when our anxieties appear in our dreams.

We are concerned about our work; it is the basis of our existence. We may love it or hate it; we may fulfill it as a duty or as a hard necessity. But anxiety grasps us whenever we feel the limits of our strength, our lack of efficiency, the struggle with our laziness, the danger of failure. We are concerned about our relationships to others. We cannot imagine living without their benevolence, their friendship, their love, their communion in body and soul. But we are worried and often in utter despair when we think about the indifference, the outbursts of anger and jealousy, the hidden and often poisonous hostility we experience in ourselves as well as in those we love. The anxiety about losing them, about having hurt them, about not being worthy of them, creeps into our hearts and makes our love restless. We are concerned about ourselves. We feel responsible for our development towards maturity, towards strength in life, wisdom in mind, and perfection in spirit. At the same time, we are striving for happiness, we are concerned about our pleasures and about "having a good time," a concern which ranks very high with us. But our anxiety strikes us when we look at ourselves in the mirror of self-scrutiny or of the judgments of others. We feel that we have made the wrong decision, that we have started on the wrong road, that we are failing before men and before ourselves. We compare ourselves with others and feel inferior to them, and we are depressed and frustrated. We believe that we have wasted our happiness either by pursuing it too eagerly and confusing happiness with pleasure or by not being courageous enough to grasp the right moment for a decision which might have brought us happiness.

We cannot forget the most natural and most universal concern of everything that lives, the concern for the preservation of life—for our daily bread. There was a time in recent history in which large groups in the Western world had almost forgotten this concern. Today, the simple concern for food and clothing and shelter is so overwhelming in the greater part of mankind that it has almost suppressed most of the other human concerns, and it has absorbed the minds of all classes of people.

But, someone may ask, do we not have higher concerns than those of our daily life? And does not Jesus Himself witness to them? When He is moved by the misery of the masses does He not consecrate the social concern which has grasped many people in our time, liberating them from many worries of their daily lives? When Jesus is moved by pity for the sick and heals them, does He not thereby consecrate the concern shared by medical and spiritual healers? When He gathers around Him a small group in order to establish community within it, does He not thereby consecrate the concern about all communal life? When He says that He has come to bear witness to the truth, does He not consecrate the concern for truth, and the passion for knowledge which is such a driving force in our time? When He is teaching the masses and His disciples, does He not consecrate the concern for learning and education? And when He tells the parables, and when He pictures the beauty of nature and creates sentences of classic perfection, does He not consecrate the concern for beauty, and the elevation of mind it gives, and the peace after the restlessness of our daily concerns?

But are these noble concerns the "one thing" that is needed and the right thing that Mary has chosen? Or are they perhaps the highest forms of what Martha represents? Are we still, like Martha, concerned about many things even when we are concerned about great and noble things?

Are we really beyond anxiety when we are socially concerned and when the mass of misery and social injustice, contrasted with our own favored position, falls upon our conscience and prevents us from breathing freely and happily while we are forced to heave the sighs of hundreds of people all over the world? And do you know the agony of those who want to heal but know it is too late; of those who want to educate and meet with stupidity, wickedness and hatred; of those who are obliged to lead and are worn out by the people's ignorance, by the ambitions of their opponents, by bad institutions and bad luck? These anxieties are greater than those about our daily life. And do you know what tremendous anxiety is connected with every honest inquiry, the anxiety about falling into error, especially when one takes new and untrod paths of thought? Have you ever experienced the almost intolerable feeling of emptiness when you turned from a great work of art to the demands, ugliness and worries of your daily life? Even this is not the "one thing" we need as Jesus indicated when He spoke of the beauties of the Temple being doomed to destruction. Modern Europe has learned that the millennia of human creativity of which it boasted were not that "one thing needful," for the monuments of these millennia now lie in ruins.

Why are the many things about which we are concerned connected with worry and anxiety? We give them our devotion, our strength, our passion and we must do so; otherwise we would not achieve anything. Why, then, do they make us restless in the deepest ground of our hearts, and why does Jesus dismiss them as not ultimately needed?

As Jesus indicates in His words about Mary, it is because they can be taken from us. They all come to an end; all our concerns are finite. In the short span of our lives many of them have already disappeared and new ones have emerged which also will disappear. Many great concerns of the past have vanished and more will come to an end, sooner or later. The melancholy law of transitoriness governs even our most passionate concerns. The anxiety of the end dwells in the happiness they give. Both the things about which we are concerned and we ourselves come to an end. There will be a moment—and perhaps it is not far away—when we shall no longer be concerned about any of these concerns, when their finitude will be revealed in the experience of our own finitude—of our own end.

But we maintain our preliminary concerns as if they were ultimate. And they keep us in their grasp if we try to free ourselves from them. Every concern is tyrannical and wants our whole heart and our whole mind and our whole strength. Every concern tries to become our ultimate concern, our god. The concern about our work often succeeds in becoming our god, as does the concern about another human being, or about pleasure. The concern about science has succeeded in becoming the god of a whole era in history, the concern about money has become an even more important god, and the concern about the nation the most important god of all. But these concerns are finite, they conflict with each other, they burden our consciences because we cannot do justice to all of them.

We may try to dismiss all concerns and to maintain a cynical unconcern. We determine that nothing shall concern us any more, except perhaps casually, but certainly not seriously. We try to be unconcerned about ourselves and others, about our work and our pleasures, about necessities and luxuries, about social and political matters, about knowledge and beauty. We may even feel that this unconcern has something heroic about it. And one thing is true: It is the only alternative to having an ultimate concern. Unconcern or ultimate concern —those are the only alternatives. The cynic is concerned, passionately concerned, about one thing, namely, his unconcern. This is the inner contradiction of all unconcern. Therefore, there is only one alternative, which is ultimate concern.

What, then, is the one thing that we need? What is the right thing that Mary has chosen? Like our story, I hesitate to answer, for almost any answer will be misunderstood. If the answer is "religion," this will be misunderstood as meaning a set of beliefs and activities.

But, as other New Testament stories show, Martha was at least as religious as Mary. Religion can be a human concern on the same level as the others, creating the same anxiety as the others. Every page of the history and psychology of religion demonstrates this. There are even special people who are supposed to cultivate this particular human concern. They are called by a highly blasphemous name: religionists—a word that reveals more about the decay of religion in our time than does anything else. If religion is the special concern of special people and not the ultimate concern of everybody, it is nonsense or blasphemy. So we ask again, what is the one thing we need? And again it is difficult to answer. If we answer "God," this will also be misunderstood. Even God can be made a finite concern, an object among other objects; in whose existence some people believe and some do not. Such a God, of course, cannot be our ultimate concern. Or we make Him a person like other persons with whom it is useful to have a relationship. Such a person may support our finite concerns, but He certainly cannot be our ultimate concern.

The one thing needed—this is the first and in some sense the last answer I can give—is to be concerned ultimately, unconditionally, infinitely. This is what Mary was. It is this that Martha felt and what made her angry, and it is what Jesus praises in Mary. Beyond this, not much has been said or could be said about Mary, and it is less than what has been said about Martha. *But Mary was infinitely concerned.* This is the one thing needed.

If, in the power and passion of such an ultimate concern, we look at our finite concerns, at the Martha sphere of life, everything seems the same and yet everything is changed. We are still concerned about all these things but differently—the anxiety is gone! It still exists and tries to return. But its power is broken; it cannot destroy us any more. He who is grasped by the one thing that is needed has the many things under his feet. They concern him but not ultimately, and when he loses them he does not lose the one thing he needs and that cannot be taken from him.

21

THE RIGHT TIME

Everything has its appointed hour,
there is a time for all things under heaven:
a time for birth, a time for death,
a time to plant and a time to uproot,
a time to kill, a time to heal,
a time to break down and a time to build,
a time to cry, a time to laugh,
a time to mourn, a time to dance,
a time to scatter and a time to gather,
a time to embrace, a time to refrain,
a time to seek, a time to lose,
a time to keep, a time to throw away,
a time to tear, a time to sew,
a time for silence and a time for speech,
a time for love, a time for hate,
a time for war, a time for peace.

ECCLESIASTES 3:1-8.

YOU HAVE READ WORDS OF A MAN
who lived about 200 years before the birth of Jesus;
a man nurtured in Jewish piety and educated in Greek
wisdom; a child of his period—a period of catastrophes

161

and despair. He expresses this despair in words of a pessimism that surpasses most pessimistic writings in world literature. Everything is in vain, he repeats many times. It is vanity, even if you were King Solomon who not only controlled the means for any humanly possible satisfaction but who also could use them with wisdom. But even such a man must say: All is in vain! We do not know the name of the writer of this book who is usually called the Preacher, although he is much more a teacher of wisdom, a practical philosopher. Perhaps we wonder how his dark considerations of man's destiny could become a Biblical book. It took indeed a long time and the overcoming of much protest before it was accepted. But finally synagogue and church accepted it; and now this book is in the Bible beside Isaiah and Matthew and Paul and John. The "all is in vain" has received Biblical authority. I believe that this authority is deserved, that it is not an authority produced by a mistake, but that it is the authority of truth. His description of the human situation is truer than any poetry glorifying man and his destiny. His honesty opens our eyes for those things which are overlooked or covered up by optimists of all kinds. So if you meet people who attack Christianity for having too many illusions tell them that their attacks would be much stronger if they allied themselves with the book of the Preacher. The very fact that this book is a part of the Bible shows clearly that the Bible is a most realistic book. And it cannot be otherwise. For only on this background the message of Jesus as the Christ has meaning. Only if we accept an honest view of the human situation, of man's old reality, can we understand the message that in

Christ a new reality has appeared. He who never has said about His life "Vanity of vanities, all is vanity" cannot honestly say with Paul, "In all these things we are more than conquerors through him who loved us."

There is a time, an appointed hour, for all things under heaven, says the Preacher. And in fourteen contrasts he embraces the whole of human existence, showing that everything has its time. What does this mean?

When the Preacher says that everything has its time, he does not forget his ever-repeated statement, "This too is vanity and striving for the wind." The fact that everything has its appointed time only confirms his tragic view. Things and actions have their time. Then they pass and other things and actions have *their* time. But nothing new comes out of this circle in which all life moves. Everything is timed by an eternal law which is above time. We are not able to penetrate into the meaning of this timing. For *us*, it is mystery and what *we* see is vanity and frustration. God's timing is hidden to us, and our toiling and timing are of no ultimate use. Any human attempt to change the rhythm of birth and death, of war and peace, of love and hate and all the other contrasts in the rhythm of life is in vain.

This is the first but it is not the whole meaning of the statement that everything has its appointed hour. If the Preacher says that there is a time to plant and a time to uproot, a time to kill, a time to heal, a time to break down and a time to build, a time to mourn and a time to dance, a time to speak and a time to be silent, he asks us to be aware of the right time, the time to do one thing and not to do another thing. After he has emphasized that everything is timed by an unsurmountable destiny, he asks us to follow this timing from above and to do our own timing according to it. As a teacher of wisdom who gives many wise rules for our acting, he requests right timing. He knows that all our timing is dependent on the timing from above, from the hidden ruler of time; but this does not exclude our acting at the right and not at the wrong moment. The whole ancient world was driven by the belief that for everything we do there is an adequate hour: If you want to build a house or to marry, if you want to travel or to begin a war—for any important enterprise—you must ask for the right moment. You must ask somebody who knows—the priest or the astrologer, the seer or the prophet. On the ground of their oracles about the good season you may or may not act. This was a belief of centuries and millennia. It was one of the strongest forces in human history, from generation to generation. The greatest men of the past waited for the oracle announcing the appointed hour. Jesus Himself says that His hour has not yet come and He went to Jerusalem when He felt that His hour *had* come.

The modern man usually does not ask for oracles. But the modern man knows of the need for timing as much as his predecessors. When in my early years in this country I had to discuss a certain project with an influential American business man he said to me, "Don't forget that the first step to a successful action is the right timing." Innumerable times, when reading about political or commercial actions, I was reminded of these words. In many conversations about activities and plans the problem of timing came up. It is one of the most manifest patterns of our culture, of our industrial civi-

lization. How does it compare with the words of the
Preacher?

When the business man spoke to me about timing he
thought of what *he* had done and what *he* would do.
He betrayed the pride of a man who knows the right
hour for his actions, who was successful in his timing,
who felt as the master of his destiny, as the creator of
new things, as the conqueror of situations. This certainty is not the mood of the Preacher. Even if the
Preacher points to the need of right timing he does
not give up his great "All is vanity." You must do it,
you must grasp the right moment, but ultimately it
does not matter. The end is the same for the wise and
the fool, for him who toils and for him who enjoys himself, the end is even the same for man and for animals.

The Preacher is first of all conscious that he *is* timed;
and he points to our timing as a secondary matter. The
modern business man is first of all conscious that *he* has
to time, and only vaguely realizes that he *is* timed. Of
course, he also is aware that he has not produced the
right time, that he is dependent on it, that he may
miss it in his calculations and actions. He knows that
there is a limit to his timing, that there are economic
forces stronger than he, that he also is subject to a final
destiny which ends all his planning. He is aware of it,
but he disregards it when he plans and acts. Quite different is the Preacher. He starts his enumeration of
things that are timed with birth and death. They are
beyond human timing. They are the signposts which
cannot be trespassed. We cannot time them and all our
timing is limited by them. This is the reason why in
the beginning of our modern era death and sin and hell

were removed from the public consciousness. While in
the Middle Ages every room, every street, and, more
important, every heart and every mind were filled with
symbols of the end, of death, it has been today a matter of bad taste even to mention death. The modern
man feels that the awareness of the end disturbs and
weakens his power of timing. He has, instead of the
threatening symbols of death, the clock in every room,
on every street, and, more important, in his mind and
in his nerves. There is something mysterious about the
clock. It determines our daily timing. Without it we
could not plan for the next hour, we could not time
any of our activities. But the clock also reminds us of
the fact that we *are* timed. It indicates the rush of our
time towards it. The voice of the clock has reminded
many people of the fact that they are timed. In an old
German night-watchman's street song every hour is an-
nounced with a special reminder. Of midnight it says:
"Twelve—that is the goal of time, give us, O God,
eternity." These two attitudes toward the clock indicate two ways of timing—the one as being timed, the
other as timing for the next hour, for today and tomorrow. What does the clock tell you? Does it point to the
hour of rising and working and eating and talking and
going to sleep? Does it point to the next appointment
and the next project? Or does it show that another day,
another week have passed, that we have become older,
that better timing is needed to use our last years for
the fulfillment of our plans, for planting and building
and finishing before it is too late? Or does the clock
make us anticipate the moment in which its voice does
not speak any more for us? Have we, the men of the

industrial age, the men who are timing every hour from day to day, the courage and the imagination of the Preacher who looks back at all *his* time and all *his* timing and calls it vanity? And if so, what about our timing? Does it not lose any meaning? Must we not say with the Preacher that it is good for man to enjoy life as it is given to him from hour to hour, but that it is better not to be born at all?

There is another answer to the question of human existence, to the question of timing and being timed. It is summed up in the words of Jesus: "The time is fulfilled and the kingdom of God is at hand." In these words, God's timing breaks into our human timing. Something new appears, answering the question of the Preacher is well as the question of the business man. We ask with all generations of thinking men: What is the meaning of the flux of time and the passing away of everything in it? What is the meaning of our toiling and planning when the end of all of us and of all our works is the same? Vanity? And this is the answer we get: Within this our time something happens that is not of our time but out of eternity, and this times *our* time! The same power which limits us in time gives eternal significance to our timing. When Jesus says that the right hour has come, that the kingdom of God is at hand, He pronounces the victory over the law of vanity. *This* hour is not subject to the circle of life and death and all the other circles of vanity. When God Himself appears in a moment of time, when He Himself subjects Himself to the flux of time, the flux of time is conquered. And if this happens in *one* moment of time, then *all* moments of time receive another significance. When the finger of the clock turns around; not one vain moment is replaced by another vain moment, but each moment says to us: The eternal is at hand in *this* moment. The moment passes, the eternal remains. Whatever in this moment, in this hour, on this day and in this short or long life-time happens has infinite significance. Our timing from moment to moment, our planning today for tomorrow, the toil of our life-time is not lost. Its deepest meaning lies not ahead where vanity swallows it, but it lies above where eternity affirms it. This is the seriousness of time and timing. Through our timing God times the coming of His kingdom; through our timing He elevates the time of vanity into the time of fulfillment. The activist who is timing with shrewdness and intuition what he has to do in his time and for his time, and for our whole activistic civilization cannot give us the answer. And the Preacher, who himself once was a most successful activist, knows that this is not an answer; he knows the vanity of our timing. And let us be honest. The spirit of the Preacher is strong today in our minds. His mood fills our philosophy and poetry. The vanity of human existence is described powerfully by those who call themselves philosophers or poets of existence. They all are the children of the Preacher, this great existentialist of his period. But neither they nor the Preacher know an answer. They know more than the men of mere acting. They know the vanity of acting and timing. They know that we *are* timed. But they do *not* know the answer either. Certainly we must act; we cannot help it. We have to time our lives from day to day. Let us do it as clearly and as successfully as the Preacher when he still followed the example of King Solomon. But let us follow him also when he saw *through* all this and realized its vanity.

Then, and then alone, are we prepared for the message of the eternal appearing in time and elevating time to eternity. Then we see in the movement of the clock not *only* the passing of one moment after the other, but also the eternal at hand, threatening, demanding, promising. Then we are able to say: "In spite"! In spite of the fact that the Preacher and all his pessimistic followers today and everywhere and at all times are right, I say yes to time and to toil and to acting. I know the infinite significance of every moment. But again in saying so we should not relapse into the attitude of the activist, not even of the Christian activist—and there are many of them, men and women in Christendom. The message of the fulfillment of time is not a green light for a new, an assumedly Christian activism. But it makes us say with Paul: "Though our outer nature is wasting away our inner nature is renewed every day—because we look not to the things that are seen but to the things that are unseen. For the things that are seen are transient, but the things that are unseen are eternal." In these words the message of the Preacher and the message of Jesus are united. All is vanity but through this vanity eternity shines into us, comes near to us, draws us to itself. When eternity calls in time, then activism vanishes. When eternity calls in time, then pessimism vanishes. When eternity times us, then time becomes a vessel of eternity. Then we become vessels of that which is eternal.

22

LOVE IS STRONGER THAN DEATH

We know that we have passed out of death into life, because we love the brethren. He who does not love remains in death.

I JOHN 3:14.

IN OUR TIME, AS IN EVERY AGE, WE NEED to see something which is stronger than death. Death has become powerful in our time, in individual human beings, in families, in nations and in mankind as a whole. Death has become powerful—that is to say that the End, the finite, and the limitations and decay of our being have become visible. For nearly a century this was concealed in Western civilization. We had become masters in our earthly household. Our control over nature, and our social planning had widened the boundaries of our being; the affirmation of life had drowned out its negation which no longer dared make itself heard, and which fled into the hidden anxiety of our hearts, becoming fainter and fainter. We forgot that we are finite, and we forgot the abyss of nothingness surrounding us. We had gathered into our barns the fruits of thousands of years of toil. All generations of men had labored so that we, the generation of fulfillment, might tread death under our feet. It was not death in the sense of the natural end of life which we thought to have destroyed, but death as a power in and over life.

170

as the Lord and master of the soul. We kept the picture of death from our children and when here and there, in our neighborhood and in the world, mortal convulsions and the End became visible, our security was not disturbed. For us these events were merely accidental and unavoidable, but they were not enough to tear off the lid which we had fastened down over the abyss of our being.

And suddenly the lid was torn off. The picture of Death appeared, unveiled, in a thousand forms. As in the late Middle Ages the figure of Death appeared in pictures and poetry, and the Dance of Death with every living being was painted and sung, so our generation —the generation of world wars, revolutions, and mass migrations—rediscovered the reality of death. We have seen millions die in war, hundreds of thousands in revolutions, tens of thousands in persecutions and systematic purges of minorities. Multitudes as numerous as whole nations still wander over the face of the earth or perish when artificial walls put an end to their wanderings. All those who are called refugees or immigrants belong to this wandering; in them is embodied a part of these tremendous events in which Death has again grasped the reins which we believed it had relinquished forever. Such people carry in their souls, and often in their bodies, the traces of death, and they will never completely lose them. You who have never taken part yourselves in this great migration must receive these others as symbols of a death which is a component element of life. Receive them as people who, by their destiny, shall remind us of the presence of the End in every moment of life and history. Receive them as symbols of the finiteness and transitoriness of every human concern, of every human life, and of every created thing.

We have become a generation of the End and those of us who have been refugees and exiles should not forget this when we have found a new beginning here or in another land. The End is nothing external. It is not exhausted by the loss of that which we can never regain: our childhood homes, the people with whom we grew up, the country, the things, the language which formed us, the goods, both spiritual and material, which we inherited or earned, the friends who were torn away from us by sudden death. The End is more than all this; it is in us, it has become our very being. We are a generation of the End and we should know that we are. Perhaps there are some who think that what has happened to them and to the whole world should now be forgotten. Is it not more dignified, truer and stronger to say "yes" to that which is our destiny, to refuse to cover the signs of the End in our lives and in our souls, to let the voice of Death be heard? Amid all the new possibilities offered to us, must we not acknowledge ourselves to be that which destiny has made us? Must we not confess that we are symbols of the End? And this End is of an age which was both great and a lie. It is the End for all finitude which always becomes a lie when it forgets that it is finite and seeks to veil the picture of death.

But who can bear to look at this picture? Only he who can look at another picture behind and beyond it —the picture of Love. For love is stronger than death. Every death means parting, separation, isolation, opposition and not participation. So it is, too, with the death of nations, the end of generations, and the atrophy of souls. Our souls become poor and disintegrate insofar as we want to be alone, insofar as we bemoan our misfortunes, nurse our despair and enjoy our bitterness, and yet turn coldly away from the physical and spiritual need of others. Love overcomes separation and creates participation in which there is more than that which the individuals involved can bring to it. Love is the infinite which is given to the finite. Therefore we love in others, for we do not merely love others, but we love the Love that is in them and which is more than their or our love. In mutual assistance what is most important is not the alleviation of need but the actualization of love. Of course, there is no love which does not want to make the other's need its own. But there is also no true help which does not spring from love and create love. Those who fight against death and disintegration through all kinds of relief agencies know this. Often very little external help is possible. And the gratitude of those who receive help is first and always gratitude for love and only afterwards gratitude for help. Love, not help, is stronger than death. But there is no love which does not become help. Where help is given without love, there new suffering grows from the help.

It is love, human and divine, which overcomes death in nations and generations and in all the horror of our time. Help has become almost impossible in the face of the monstrous powers which we are experiencing. Death is given power over everything finite, especially in our period of history. But death is given no power over love. Love is stronger. It creates something new out of the destruction caused by death; it bears everything and overcomes everything. It is at work where the power of death is strongest, in war and persecution and homelessness and hunger and physical death itself. It is omnipresent and here and there, in the smallest and most hidden ways as in the greatest and most visible ones, it rescues life from death. It rescues each of us, for love is stronger than death.

23

UNIVERSAL SALVATION

*Now from the sixth hour there was darkness over
all the land until the ninth hour. And about the ninth
hour Jesus cried with a loud voice, "Eli, Eli, la'ma
sabach-tha'ni?" that is, "My God, my God, why hast
thou forsaken me?"*

*And Jesus cried again with a loud voice and
yielded up his spirit. And behold, the curtain of the
temple was torn in two, from top to bottom; and the
earth shook, and the rocks were split; the tombs also
were opened, and many bodies of the saints who
had fallen asleep were raised, and coming out of the
tombs after his resurrection they went into the holy
city and appeared to many. When the centurion and
those who were with him, keeping watch over Jesus,
saw the earthquake and what took place, they were
filled with awe, and said, "Truly this was a son of
God!"*

MATTHEW 27:45-46; 50-54.

IN THE STORIES OF THE CRUCIFIXION
the agony and the death of Jesus are connected with
a group of events in nature: Darkness covers the land;
the curtain of the temple is torn in two; the earth is

175

shaken and the bodies of saints rise out of their graves. Nature, with trembling, participates in the decisive event of history. The sun veils its head; the temple makes the gesture of mourning; the foundations of the earth are moved; the tombs are opened. Nature is in an uproar because something is happening which concerns the universe.

Since the time of the evangelists, wherever the story of Golgotha has been told as the turning event in the world-drama of salvation, the role nature played in this drama has also been told. Painters of the crucifixion have used all their artistic power to express the darkness over the land in almost unnatural colors. I remember my own earliest impression of Good Friday—the feeling of the mystery of the divine suffering, first of all, through the compassion of nature. And so did the centurion, the first pagan who witnessed for the Crucified. Filled with awe, with numinous dread, he understood in a naive-profound way that something more had happened than the death of a holy and innocent man.

We should *not* ask whether clouds or a dust storm darkened the sun on a special day of a special year, whether an earthquake happened in Palestine just at that hour, whether the curtain before the holy of holies in the temple at Jerusalem had to be repaired or whether the raised bodies of the saints died again. But we *should* ask whether we are able to feel with the evangelists and the painters, with the children and the Roman soldiers, that the event at Golgotha is one which concerns the universe, including all nature and all history. With this question in our mind let us look at the signs reported by our evangelist.

The sun veiled its face because of the depth of evil and shame which it saw under the Cross. But the sun also veiled its face because its power over the world had ceased once and forever in these hours of its darkness. The great shining and burning god of everything that lives on earth, the sun who was praised and feared and adored by innumerable human beings during thousands and thousands of years, had been deprived of its divine power when *one* human being in ultimate agony maintained His unity with that which is greater than the sun. Since those hours of darkness it is manifest that not the sun, but a suffering and struggling soul which cannot be broken by all the powers of the universe is the image of the Highest, and that the sun can only be praised in the way of St. Francis, who called it our brother, but not our god.

"The curtain of the temple was torn in two." The temple tore its gown as the mourners did because He, to whom the temple belonged more than to anybody else, was thrown out and killed by the servants of the temple. But the temple—and with it, all temples on earth—also complained of its own destiny. The curtain which made the temple a holy place, separated from other places, lost its separating power. He who was expelled as blaspheming the temple, had cleft the curtain and opened the temple for everybody, for every moment. *This* curtain cannot be mended any more, although there are priests and ministers and pious people who try to mend it. They will *not* succeed because He, for whom every place was a sacred place, a place where God is present, has been brought on the Cross in the name of the holy place. When the curtain of the temple was torn in two, God judged religion and rejected temples. After this moment temples and churches can only mean places of concentration on the holy which is the ground and the meaning of every place. And like the temple, the earth was judged at Golgotha. Trembling and shaking the earth participated in the agony of the man on the Cross and in the despair of all those who had seen in Him the beginning of the new eon. Trembling and shaking the earth proved that it is not the motherly ground on which we can safely build our houses and cities, our cultures and religious systems. Trembling and shaking the earth pointed to another ground on which the earth itself rests: the self-surrendering love on which all earthly powers and values concentrate their hostility and which they cannot conquer. Since the hour when Jesus uttered a loud cry and breathed His last and the rocks were split, the earth ceased to be the foundation of what we build on her. Only insofar as it has a deeper ground, can it stand; only insofar as it is rooted in the same foundation in which the Cross is rooted, can it last.

And the earth not only ceases to be the solid ground of life; she also ceases to be the lasting cave of death. Resurrection is not something added to the death of Him who is the Christ; but it is implied in His death, as the story of the resurrection before the resurrection, indicates. No longer is the universe subjected to the law of death out of birth. It is subjected to a higher law, to the law of life out of death by the death of Him who represented eternal life. The tombs were opened and bodies were raised when one man in whom God was present without limit committed His spirit into His Father's hands. Since this moment the universe is no longer what it was; nature has received another meaning; history is transformed and you and I are no more, and should not be any more, what we were before.